Pondering My Journey

At Age 90

Quin Sherrer

Pondering My Journey

Copyright @ Quin Sherrer 2024

All rights reserved. No part of this publication may be reproduced, stored in a retrieval system, or transmitted in any form or by any means—for example, electronic, photocopies, recording—without the prior written permission of the author or publisher. The exception is brief quotations in printed reviews.

Printed in the United States of America.

Unless otherwise indicated, Scripture quotations are taken from the Holy Bible, New International Version, Registered. Copyright 1973, 1978, 1984, 2011. By Biblica, Inc. TMU. All rights reserved worldwide, www.Zondervan.com.

Scripture quotations marked AMP are taken from the Amplified® Bible, Copyright © 2015 by The Lockman Foundation. Used by permission. www.lockman.org.

Scripture quotations marked AMPC are from the Amplified Bible, copyright 1954, 1958, 1962, 1964, 1965, 1987 by The Lockman Foundation. www.lockman.org.

Scripture quotations marked ASV are from The American Standard Version of the Holy Bible (in the Public Domain).

Scripture quotations marked ESV are from The ESV® Bible (The Holy Bible, English Standard Version®), © 2001 by Crossway, a publishing ministry of Good News Publishers. Used by permission. All rights reserved.

Scripture quotations marked KJV are taken from the King James Version of the Bible.

Scripture quotations marked MSG are taken from The Message. Copyright © 1993, 1994, 1995, 1996, 2000, 2001, 2002. Used by permission of NavPress Publishing Group.

Scripture quotations marked NASB are from The New American Standard Bible, copyright 1960, 1962, 1963, 1968, 1971, 1972, 1973, 1975, 1977, 1995 by The Lockman Foundation.

Scripture quotations marked NKJV are from the New King James Version. Registered. Copyright 1982 by Thomas Nelson, Inc. All rights reserved.

Scripture quotations marked TLB are taken from The Living Bible, copyright © 1971 by Tyndale House Foundation. Used by permission of Tyndale House Publishers, Carol Stream, Illinois 60188. All rights reserved.

Scripture quotations marked TPT are from The Passion Translation®. Copyright © 2017, 2018, 2020 by Passion & Fire Ministries, Inc. Used by permission. All rights reserved. ThePassionTranslation.com.

Scripture quotations identified YLT are from the Young's Literal Translation 1989. All rights reserved.

Content edit by Sherry Anderson.

Copy-editing and formatting by Désirée Schroeder.

Cover design by Eric Schroeder.

Notice: Some names and locations have been changed to protect the privacy of persons involved. Any resemblance to people you know by these names is entirely coincidental. Footnotes are given whenever possible from material researched from books, news media and/or Internet searches. Some are from personal interviews or personal experience.

All rights reserved.

ISBN: 9798322710189

Imprint: Independently published

To My Faithful Praying Friends

With gratitude for your loving friendship and diligent prayer coverage for me over the years, I honor you:

Faye, Sally, Jeanette, Mary Jo, Beth, JoNell, Ceci, Dorothea, Jane, Kate, Brenda, Sherry, Lori, Bee, Kerry, Anne, Denise, Lilia, Mary, Tracey, Elizabeth, Linda, Mary Beth, Suzanne, Susan, Ann, Nancy, Tes, Cara, Kay, Dee, Cindy, Ruthanne, Sherry Ruth, Quinett, Dutch, Chuck, Don, Michael, George, Bob, Joe, Brian, Ken, David, and Mark.

Thanks to Editors and Publishers in My Writing Journey

Ann Spangler, Don Cooper, Kim Bangs, Jane Campbell, Evelyn Bence, Jane Hansen Hoyt, Gwen Weising, Bert Ghezzi, Kyle Duncan, Bill Greig III, and all others.

Thanks for Photos

Thanks to Mary Jo Pierce for some of the photos included in this book.

"I remember the days of old; I meditate on all that you have done; I ponder the work of your hands." (Psalm 143:5 ESV)

On Flyleaf of My Bible:

He that formed me in the womb
He shall guide me to the tomb;
All my times shall ever be
Ordered by His wise decree.
—John Ryland (1753-1825)

A Psalm of Life

Life is real! Life is earnest!
And the grave is not the goal;
Dust thou art, to dust returnest,
Was not spoken of the soul.
—Henry Wadsworth Longfellow

Journey—"Life is about the journey, not the destination."—Ralph Waldo Emerson

"It's special people we meet along life's road who help us appreciate the journey."—Hallmark card

Ponder—to reflect deeply on events, to consider, to mull over, think over carefully, to ruminate, to let lingering thoughts unfold.

A Blog—a record of someone's thoughts, experiences, opinions; often personal reflections, appearing on the Internet for people to read.

Memory—is a way of holding onto the things you love, the things you are, and the things you never want to lose.—Anon.

Remember, remembrance—"To remember is a normal part of the activity of the human mind. When, however, God is the one who is remembered in prayer and ritual, or, when it is believed by the faithful that God himself is actually remembering his own relation to his people, then 'to remember' with its appropriate nouns becomes a special verb in the religious vocabulary of Israel and the church of God."[1]

Tell Others: "Telling to the generation to come the praises of the LORD, And His strength and His wonderful works that He has done." (Psalm 78:4 NKJV)

Writing: Rudyard Kipling helped us appreciate the importance of words—especially when writing or telling a story.

> I keep six honest men
> (They taught me all I knew)
> Their names are What and Why and When
> And How and Where and Who.

---

[1] Baker's Evangelical Dictionary of Biblical Theology https://www.biblestudytools.com/dictionary/remember/ (accessed Feb. 1, 2023)

Table of Contents

INTRODUCTION 1

PART ONE: THANKS & APPRECIATION 3

    THE BEGINNING OF MY LIFE 3
    JUST ONE ROOM TODAY 4
    JOURNEY INTO ANOTHER YEAR 6
    SOJOURNING ON EARTH 8

PART TWO: MY YOUTHFUL YEARS 13

    ONE COTTON PICKING DAY 13
    REUNIONS AT GRANDMOTHER'S HOUSE 15
    DEAR OLD SCHOOL DAYS 17
    AN UNEXPECTED MIRACLE 21
    PRAYERS FROM MY YOUTH 23
    A CRITICAL LIFE CHANGE 23
    INTERRUPTIONS DURING KOREAN WAR 26

PART THREE: THE ADULT YEARS 29

    MEETING A HUSBAND 29
    PRAYER FOR A HUSBAND 36
    USING OUR HANDS 37

PART FOUR: MOTHERHOOD YEARS 41

    MOTHER TO YOUNG CHILDREN 41
    HELP, LORD—IT'S FALLING APART 41
    LETTER TO MY LAST FIRST GRADER 43
    OUT-OF-THE-ORDINARY DAYS 44
    TALKING TOYS 45
    GET OUT OF HIS WAY 47
    MY HOPE WITH HIS FROG 49
    HOPING MY CHILDREN REMEMBER 51
    THEIR GRANDMOTHER'S LEGACY OF LOVE 53
    BECOMING A GRANDMOTHER, MYSELF 56

FROM THE MOUTHS OF GRANDCHILDREN	59
FRAMED ON MY GRANDMOTHER WALL OF PHOTOS	61
AN ODE TO A GARAGE	61

PART FIVE: INFLUENCERS ... 63

PURPOSEFULLY INFLUENCING FOR GOOD	63
BE A PARTICIPANT IN LIFE	65
TRIBUTE TO PASTOR PETER LORD	68
WEAR YOUR OWN SHOES	73
APPRECIATE DUTCH SHEETS	76
CATCHING WHAT WAS TAUGHT	81
PEOPLE IN MINISTRY WHOM I HEARD SPEAK OR KNEW PERSONALLY	84

PART SIX: MENTORING OTHERS ... 85

KEEPER FRIENDS ARE TREASURES	85
JOANNE'S LESSONS	92
MENTORING LESSONS LAST LONG	95
AN EXTRA CHILD TO LOVE	96
LET US MENTOR AND INFLUENCE OTHERS	99

PART SEVEN: SPIRITUAL REFLECTIONS ... 103

HOLY SPIRIT'S VISITATION	103
CHRIST, THE HOPE OF GLORY	109
A BOUQUET OF FLOWERS	111
LIFE IN LOCKDOWN DURING PANDEMIC	113
VISUAL REMINDERS HELP US FOCUS	116
QUOTES N' NOTES ON QUIN'S WRITING OFFICE WALL	116
A PRAYER FOR RIGHT THINGS	117
MY BEAN PATCH PRAYER BOARD	117
BE HOSPITABLE—NO GRUMBLING	118
PRAYER ANSWERS WITH ANGELIC HELP	121
SPEAK WORDS OF HOPE	123
LET'S LAUGH MORE	125

PART EIGHT: BOOK WRITING—WORK BUT FUN ... 129

PART NINE: WORLD ADVENTURES ... 135

OTHER ADVENTURES	140
OTHER WORLDWIDE TRIPS WITH HUSBAND	142
MY EXPERIENCES	144
TELEVISION, RADIO, AND RETREATS	147
WRONG PLACE	152
SURPRISE AIRPLANE ENCOUNTERS	152
SCOTLAND SIGHTS AND INSIGHTS	156
A FORTY-FIVE YEAR REUNION	159

PART TEN: LESSONS FROM THOSE WHO LIVED BEFORE US … 163

A MOTHER ENTERS HEAVEN	163
MY WIDOW'S LESSON	166
BURYING LOVED ONES DURING PANDEMIC	168
ROOTS AND HERITAGE FROM GRANDPARENTS	170
JOINING GENERATIONS IN A CEMETERY	173
MY FOREFATHER WAS A CHRISTIAN	177

PART ELEVEN: LIVING YOUR DASH WELL … 179

FINISHING YOUR RACE	179
JESUS IN THE OPERATING ROOM	182
A SURPRISE DIAGNOSIS	184
THE FUTURE	187
INVITE JESUS INTO YOUR LIFE	188
OLD AGE	189
AMERICA NEEDS OUR SAVIOR	190

PART TWELVE: FRIENDS PONDERING THEIR JOURNEY WITH QUIN … 191

QUIN'S BIOGRAPHY & BOOK LIST … 207

BIOGRAPHY OF QUIN SHERRER	207
BOOKS BY QUIN SHERRER AND RUTHANNE GARLOCK	209
BOOKS BY QUIN SHERRER	209
BIBLES CONTRIBUTED TO BY QUIN SHERRER	210
OTHER BOOKS CONTRIBUTED TO BY QUIN SHERRER	210

Introduction

This book is a combination of reflections from my various seasons of life, spanning 90 years. Some from my childhood, others from my early motherhood. Most of my journey has been spent in my beloved home state of Florida. Some of these are from my long-ago published pieces in newspapers, magazines, or books. Others are from blogs I have written in more recent years for my website, even during the days of the pandemic.

Please forgive me if some of the times I write about offend you, but I speak of things that I experienced or observed. And yes, I pondered a lot. While some are on a serious note, I hope others make you laugh. I pray many will cause you to thank our Creator for your experiences also. And hopefully cause you to ponder your own life's journey and challenge you to share them with others too.

Journey: There are almost 100 references to journey in the King James version of the Bible. For example, in Numbers 33 the "stages" of the Israelites' journey as they came out of Egypt are listed specifically.

Part One: Thanks & Appreciation

I am forever grateful to Ruthanne Garlock who co-labored with me to write 20 books starting in 1988. I authored an additional 11 books starting in 1986. See a list of them all at the end of this book.

I am appreciative and indebted to Sherry Anderson, my "spiritual daughter" for several decades, for her editing expertise on this book intended for family and friends. And to her precious daughter Désirée Anderson Schroeder, whom I have loved since she was a child, who did further editing and formatting. Both of these women have enriched my life with their talents and prayers. May God Himself "repay their work and a full reward be given them by the Lord" (See Ruth 2:12). And I'm grateful for Désirée's husband, Eric, who designed the cover and edited photos in the book.

And to my former pastor and cherished friend, Dutch Sheets, and his precious wife, Ceci, who have prayed and stood with me through trials and triumphs in my later years, I am truly thankful.

Now let's begin to look back, remembering each day is part of the journey.

The Beginning of My Life

The year I was born, 1933, was said to be the worst year of the Depression with unemployment at 25 percent. Droughts stripped topsoil, causing dust storms and of course, food shortages. Thousands of men traveled the rails looking for work. With the banking system under great strain, the government passed an act to try and stop people from withdrawing their money.

A year's wages averaged $1,550. A laborer, if he could find a job, made about $20 a week. You could rent a house for $18 a month or buy one for about $5,750. Or if you could afford it, a Plymouth car sold for $445. Bread cost seven cents, a gallon of gas ten cents, Franklin D. Roosevelt had become president of the United States, and Adolf Hitler, the chancellor of Germany, opened the first concentration camp in Dachau.

I have lived under 15 American presidents and in three different states, in nine decades between the "then" and "now" of my life. At our Tallahassee high school graduation party, the church's youth pastor asked us to share what our dreams were for our future. What were our goals? Our hopes? My answer was simple. "To be a wife, mother, and a writer." And the Lord graciously granted that request.

Prayer: Heavenly Father, I thank You that my parents and grandparents made it through the Depression despite their many challenges. I am grateful for the lessons they learned and passed on to their four children as a result. I am grateful too for long life You have given me and the hundreds of people I have had the privilege to meet, many of whom have enriched my life. Amen.

Scripture: For He Himself has said, "I will never leave you nor forsake you." (Hebrews 13:5b NKJV)

Just One Room Today

One room. That's where I live. In it I pray and commune with God. Write blogs for my website. Sleep when insomnia does not grab me. Connect on prayer calls for America. Mentor by phone. Attend church online. Stay connected with friends through email, phone, or texting. Get my entertainment on television. Brew my cup of coffee. One room. Just one room.

Now I am 90 years old. In my home, three generations of us live peacefully and with love and respect for one another. They cook for me, run my errands, get my mail.

My times of hospitality, entertaining, and holding prayer meetings in my home have ceased. But that's not so bad—good memories of those days make me smile in appreciation for all who have passed through our homes in the past. I am grateful for what God helped me do.

One week alone, more than 100 people signed our guest book. We had Glory Parties, Writing Seminars, Prayer Meetings, Teen Get-togethers, Slumber Parties, Car Repair Sessions, and all kinds of birthday and holiday gatherings. We did not have large houses but when our kids were growing up, we had a screen porch and once in a while we fed as many as 40 out there.

My days of travelling to speak have stopped. But, hey, I have had the privilege of going to 26 countries—speaking in 12 nations and 47 states and on more than 375 radio and television stations. Using the talent God gave me, I have tried to be faithful with it, writing or co-authoring 31 books and hundreds of articles for newspapers and magazines.

My life has been full. Over 50 years of marriage to one man, three children who love the Lord, and six grandkids. So, this grandmother prays!

The other day two friends picked me up and we spent three hours driving and praying over our city and the nearby military base—stopping at strategic spots to pray and take communion in remembrance of Him who shed His blood for us. I left my One Room for a prayer assignment from God. And I loved it!

Just the other night I did a Zoom teaching to 15 women in Birmingham, Alabama on my book *Cast Your Shadow: Influence on Purpose*. I love this technology which has allowed me to teach on my book topics across the nation.

PONDERING MY JOURNEY

Old age is not what I imagined. Serious health issues. I am depending on God, doctors, vitamins, and meds to help me keep on living. But here I sit at a computer at seven on a Tuesday morning turning this out—so there you have it. My life summary. And I fully intend to fulfill and finish my God-ordained destiny. The assignment over the years just continues to change a bit.

So, today is another new day, another week, another opportunity to encourage and pray for someone without ever leaving my One Room. Today I hope it might even be you!

Blessings and have a happy fulfilling day. *Quin*

Journey into Another Year

As we enter a new year, we can seize it as an opportunity for a fresh start. Expecting wonderful surprises. But we can also reflect on whatever good we experienced in the year past.

What do you treasure most about what's behind you? What do you look forward to doing, seeing, hearing, just "being" you in the year ahead?

Arthur Gordon, in *Return to Wonder,* challenges us to look for and treasure even the unexpected. And yes, to look back with gratitude.

"Life is such a mysterious and complicated journey," he writes. "Most travelers, I think, look back in terms of things they see on their journeys. But I believe the things you remember longest are often the sudden, unexpected, surprising little happenings that jolt you for half a second, out of the rut you are in, or perhaps even out of the self you normally are."[2]

That really speaks to me! Sudden, unexpected, surprising little happenings. Wow! They do have a way of jolting me out of a rut.

---

[2] Arthur Gordon, *Return to Wonder: Recapture a Childlike Fascination with Daily Life*, A Guidepost book. (Nashville, TN: Broadman & Holman Publishers, 1996), 94.

Can you identify too? When you recall memories, what pops into your mind? Experiences—yours or those of other people? How God played a special role in your life? What causes you to wonder the most? Causes you to ponder?

"Driving yourself to return to wonder is one thing, doing it is another," admits Gordon. "The trouble lies not in the lack of memories, but in the abundance of them. There are so many that the choice becomes difficult... In a way I think the more commonplace the happening the better. Then you have to work a bit to see the miraculous and let it come through. Perhaps what you have to do is add astonishment to ordinary cause-and-effect." Gordon says.[3]

When I go to last year's memory bank, I have a tendency to recall the sadness rather than the good.

For instance, just days before Christmas, three of my precious long-time friends died. They all went to heaven and are enjoying a glorious life now. But oh, the heartache I feel as I miss talking with them via phone. So, I decided when I talk with their surviving spouses, I can help us both laugh by recalling something funny or remarkable that each said or did. And I marvel at the wonder.

I even helped one husband decide what to engrave on his wife's gravestone. JoAnne had travelled with me as an intercessor throughout this nation and Europe when I spoke on my book topics—so he added PRAYER WARRIOR to her gravestone. He and I have spent a great deal of time swapping stories about her remarkable gift of leading people to salvation—to accept Jesus as Savior. And we repeated her clever sayings which she called her "blurbs."

As Christians we can pause at the beginning of this new year to renew our dedication to our Savior Jesus Christ. To praise God for

---

[3] Ibid., 67.

our life and anchor our trust in His promises for our future as we continue our life's journey. Asking the Holy Spirit, too, to guide and teach us.

Let's not forget to look for wonder even in the commonplace!

Prayer: Heavenly Father, Thank You for our very life itself—and for the way You have helped us on our earth's journey. We praise You for what You have done for us and through us. May we remember to be Your hands outstretched to those You put in our path. We pray in the name of Jesus. Amen.

Scriptures: "O give thanks to the LORD, for He is good! For His mercy endures forever." (Psalm 136:1 NASB)

"O God, You have taught me from my youth; And to this day I declare Your wondrous works. Now also when I am old and grayheaded, O God, do not forsake me, Until I declare Your strength to this generation, Your power to everyone who is to come." (Psalm 71:17-18 NKJV)

"These are the stages of the journeys of the Israelites, by which they came out of the land of Egypt by their [tribal] armies, under the leadership of Moses and Aaron. Moses recorded their points of departure, as the Lord commanded, stage by stage; and these are their journeys according to their points of departure." (Numbers 33:1-2 AMP)

Quin's note: I had the privilege of sitting under Arthur Gordon, one of the writing instructors at Guideposts Magazine Writers Workshop, some years ago and his many books continue to inspire readers.

Sojourning on Earth

We are just sojourners on this earth, aren't we? What a journey it has been! And continues to be.

Everyone wants to live a long life, but no one wants to grow old. Most of us have heard that statement many times. However, we do grow old. But how do we or others view us when we do?

"Judaism appreciates gray hair as a symbol of experience, character, and wisdom. My father always spoke of his love for each of his gray hairs. Each served as an eloquent reminder coming at him from his mirror each morning, he said, of how important it was to make every present moment count," writes Rabbi Daniel Lapin.[4]

Just because we turn another leaf on the calendar does not mean that we have finished our destiny. Indeed, no. We can still influence and help others in meaningful ways. But are they willing?

Will you, dear reader, consider allowing someone older to share your journey with you? Have you considered letting someone of the older generation into your life?

There are 54 million people in our nation who are 65 and older. And almost 15 million of them are widows and widowers, according to the latest data.[5] What a rich deposit of talent and skill many of those "mature citizens" have that they could share with younger ones. Many are in good health and ready to share out of their experiences, to impart to others.

One day after I reached "senior citizen age," I went to a new doctor and asked if he could help me with a health issue. After some tests, he studied the results on a chart. Through piercing eyes, he asked me a pointed question.

"What? Do you want to live forever?"

"I have not finished my race yet," I answered him.

---

[4] Rabbi Daniel Lapin, *Thou Shall Prosper*. (Hoboken, New Jersey: John Wiley & Sons, Inc., 2002), 219.
[5] www: census.gov/topic/population

"Well, no one has ever told me that," he replied.

"I am telling you then." I said in an agitated tone of voice.

I have since told a few more doctors the same thing. No, I have not finished my race yet. Yes, I know I will not live forever on earth. But I will in heaven. Today I am still alive! On earth. And so are you!

The Bible highlights journeys of great younger ones who were strongly influenced by a godly older mentor. Joshua learned his leadership roles by following Moses. Elisha gained from the prophet Elijah. Esther listened and obeyed her elder relative, Mordecai, which saved the lives of thousands of Jews. Timothy became Paul's spiritual son. And on it goes.

So, couldn't you be open to ask a more mature Christian to help guide you on your life's journey? To serve the Lord even more effectively? I am an advocate of inviting older ones into your life because it worked so great for me. Mary Jo, Margaret, Dot, Pastor Peter Lord, and other seniors contributed greatly to my Christian growth when I was young. I gladly invited them to do so.

Look around you. There is possibly a man or woman in their sunset years who would be happy to offer you some down-to-earth common-sense advice. Or even just pray for your family on a regular basis—in their own prayer closet.

And it just might make your sojourn on earth—this temporary stay— much more interesting, rewarding, and memorable!

Prayer: Father, may I finish well Your plan and intention for me and stay willing for others to help me accomplish it. I thank You in advance. In the name of Jesus, I pray. Amen.

Scriptures: "O God, you have helped me from my earliest childhood—and I have constantly testified to others of the wonderful things you do. And now that I am old and gray, don't forsake me. Give me time to tell this new generation (and their children too) about all your mighty miracles." (Psalm 71:17-18 TLB)

"Direct me, Yahweh, throughout my journey so I can experience your plans for my life. Reveal the life-paths that are pleasing to you." (Psalm 25:4 TPT)

"Hear my prayer, O Lord, and listen to my cry; Do not be silent at my tears; For I am Your temporary guest, A sojourner like all my fathers." (Psalm 39:12 AMP)

"They will live long lives, like age-old trees, and my chosen ones will enjoy to the fullest the work of their hands throughout their lives." (Isaiah 65:20 TPT)

"Is not wisdom found among the aged? Does not long life bring understanding?" (Job 12:12)

Part Two: My Youthful Years

One Cotton Picking Day

If we are honest, I imagine all of us can recall just one memorable day that was a game-changer for us. A day that made such an impression that even now as we ponder on it, we are glad for the lesson we learned—and never forgot. What was yours?

Mine happened when I was in the fifth grade in a small town in Texas.

World War II was in full force in the 1940s, and there was a shortage of cotton pickers to gather cotton necessary for making uniforms and other clothing. So, on this particular Saturday, we kids volunteered and boarded buses at the school which transported us to a cotton field on the outskirts of town.

I had never even seen anyone pick cotton. But like the other students, I thought it was a good way to earn some money. As the smallest in the class, I was the least likely to make much cash picking cotton. The boss gave us instructions for how to pick, and we set out to our allotted rows, laughing giddily because this seemed like fun.

Before long as the sun began to bear down, I wiped beads of sweat off my face with my sleeve. Pretty soon my hands were so pricked from the cotton bolls, they started bleeding. Soon after nine

PONDERING MY JOURNEY

o'clock, hunger pains drove me to gobble up the baked sweet potato Mom had packed for my lunch.

When our sacks became too heavy to drag any longer, we drug them to the scales where the bookkeeper weighed and recorded our poundage so he could later tally up our earnings. I kept going back and forth to have my pitiful little bit of cotton weighed.

After we had picked for what seemed like forever, I could barely walk to the bus to ride back to school that late afternoon. For my one cotton picking day I earned 50 cents. Fifty cents, mind you! I didn't consider it much for my hard work.

At home that night I doctored my scratched and bleeding hands, rubbed my aching neck, and decided I'd find something less painful to do with my hands when I grew up. Yes, I decided then and there that I would learn to use my hands on a typewriter.

I also determined to always maintain a deep appreciation and compassion for those who work with their hands doing tough outdoor jobs—farming, building, logging, climbing poles. On and on I thought about various jobs.

Later when I was grown, I used my hands to peck on a typewriter. And I even passed a typing speed test that qualified me to work for the Navy in Washington, D.C. Over the next decades, my magazine and newspaper assignments and book research took me to other nations, and I sometimes lugged my trusty portable typewriter with me.

Not too long ago, while visiting relatives in Mississippi, I saw a giant machine whip through a cotton field in nothing flat, gathering rows of the white fluffy cotton, rolling the loads into a big ball, and finally dropping them onto the ground for later pickup. This time-saving invention fascinated me. And it reminded me once again of myself as a skinny fifth grader who probably didn't even deserve the 50 cents I got paid on that Cotton Picking Day.

A few months before I turned 90, my daughter drove me to the town where I was born. I had not been there since my birth. She pulled over beside a cotton field on the edge of town and jumped out of the car. Grabbing a few stray handfuls of the soft white fluff that had blown to the roadside, she handed them to me. "A cotton souvenir," she said, laughing.

I thought back to my "lesson learned" on my one cotton picking day when I got a real appreciation for all who work hard to make a living, no matter what their occupation. Now as I type on this fancy laptop computer, I can see that cotton sample on my desk.

My take-away is this: we need each other! I appreciate and applaud people who are faithful in their job—any job—because they are using their abilities, skills, and experience to help many of us accomplish our own destiny.

Prayer: Father, Thank You, Lord, for all who work and make an honest living. Amen.

Scriptures: "Whatever your hand finds to do, do it with all your might." (Ecclesiastes 9:10a NKJV)

"I have set the Lord always before me; Because He is at my right hand I shall not be moved." (Psalm 16:8 NKJV)

Reunions at Grandmother's House

Do you have a favorite memory of your grandparents? Mine is about my grandmother Nanny's unique way of getting the cousins to talk and dream of their future.

Grandmother's home. It always seemed the same, but it was half a dozen different houses in whatever state Granddaddy happened to be serving as a pastor. He was a country preacher and lived in the middle of his cluster of small churches. The big old parsonages seemed the same to a little girl who only saw them once a year.

PONDERING MY JOURNEY

The house usually needed a new coat of paint, or some new roof shingles, or a sagging back step repaired. But each home had an ample porch and two rockers waiting.

They lived in a variety of places, from the windswept plains of Texas to the rich fertile farmlands of Mississippi, from the slick red clay hills of Alabama to the marshlands of Northwest Florida. And in each place, the church provided their house.

The big porches were sanctuaries for the boy cousins on summer nights as they stretched out on quilt pallets and swatted mosquitoes and swapped tales. Upstairs, the girl cousins drew straws to see who would end up in the big feather bed and who would sleep on the extra mattress laid out in the hallway.

Family reunions at Grandmother's were a special summer thing. You didn't dare miss them. Indoors, the kitchen buzzed with sounds and smells that drifted outdoors to tempt the youngsters pitching horseshoes and climbing chinaberry trees. Or gathering tomatoes and cucumbers from the kitchen garden.

Food at Grandmother's—always heaps of fried chicken to be devoured with fresh vegetables and cornbread sticks. Grownups sat in the dining room and children on the back porch. The bowing of heads, the giving of thanks, the noisy chatter while we ate. Then, the cranking of the ice cream freezer.

The cousins got reacquainted while shelling a bushel of black-eyed peas. Grandmother Nanny saw to that! All could catch up on life since last year in the time it took to shell them. Boys and girls shared their big dreams. They wanted to grow up to be lawyers, teachers, writers, moms, and dads. And they did.

One year, long after my grandmother's death, some cousins gathered at my mom's house and caught up with stories of our lives while shelling peas for her. Several of us glanced down at our hands, thankful that we were still able to do menial tasks like our grandmother. We talked about how crippled her hands became after the bus wreck injuries left one hand so badly affected, she could no longer play the piano. But she could still sit on the back porch and visit with us while we shelled away at those peas—encouraging us to talk about what we wanted to do when we were grown up.

Grandmother's house. Plump feather beds, lumpy Duncan Phyfe couches, tiny china teacups, lemon drop candy she gave us to suck between meals, and an endless parade of grandchildren through her house in summer.

Golden yesterdays. In the country. At the parsonage. With Grandmother.

Times have changed—become modern. My children's cousins don't gather like we did—they are too busy with careers and live so far apart. And they buy their garden vegetables from supermarket frozen-food shelves. They have no idea what memory-making times they are missing by not experiencing shared dreams and secrets at a back porch pea-shelling session.

Prayer: Lord, I am grateful as I recall great bygone days and I appreciate even more the sacrifice of time and finances our parents made to get the families together at their own parents' home. Our parents who survived the Great Depression and World War II consequences were giving us the precious gift of family closeness. Thank You for providing for them so they could do that. Amen.

Scripture: "Telling to the generation to come the praises of the LORD, And His strength and His wonderful works that He has done." (Psalm 78:4 NKJV)

Dear Old School Days

I am a profound memory cherisher. Aren't you? It is not that I long for the days when I was a schoolgirl, only that I want to pass some of their significance to my grandchildren's generation. Do you ever sit down and share your bygone days with your younger generation?

PONDERING MY JOURNEY

Born during the Depression, my siblings and I began our education during the war-clouded years of World War II. We and our classmates sang, "Over There," "Anchors Away," and "Coming in on a Wing and a Prayer." We learned to read from the look-say method, reading from Dick and Jane books. Before we even reported to our classrooms each morning, we all gathered in the auditorium for the Pledge of Allegiance to the Flag. Then a teacher read a Bible Scripture and prayed for our day—in our public school.

We walked nearly a mile to school, crossing a railroad track to get there. No one had to explain why there was no extra gas to transport us to school. A war was on.

The war affected us as it did all the nation—shortages of goods, primarily. My dad served as one of the civil patrol wardens who patrolled the city at night to make sure that all houses were darkened by shades—no light shining anywhere. We got our news from one radio in the house and listened intently to war news when we could. Three of my uncles in the military were serving overseas.

One Sunday night in December during those war years, our car was stolen from the church parking lot while we attended services inside. Our parents had hidden our Christmas gifts—mostly just clothes—in the car trunk. It was a very slim Christmas that year. Months later when the car was found, there were no tires on it, no gas ration stamps in the glove compartment and no presents in the trunk. From then on Dad borrowed a car from a friend when he needed one.

Finally, when the war ended, so did our air raid practice, buying war bonds, and slicing our loaves of bread. We now sang such tongue-wagging songs as "Mares Eat Oats," and a western tune which pleaded, "Don't Fence Me In." In English classes, the Holy Bible was often referred to, and we began studying Shakespeare in a simplified form.

Quin, the oldest, with her siblings, Ann, James, and Arthur. Childhood in 1947.

In high school, we were introduced to a Southern activity called Sadie Hawkins Day. Classes were canceled but students came to school anyway. Dressed in their cleverest costumes to resemble comic book characters from Li'l Abner, the gals ran races to catch the guys. Students enjoyed apple cider for sipping, box lunches for eating, three-legged races, and hayrides on wagons pulled by mules. That night there was a "Sox Hop"—far more fun than a sophisticated junior-senior prom. Besides it was a low-cost way to enjoy a school dance.[6]

Then there was Armistice Day. On November 11th at precisely 11:00 a.m. each year, a parade made its way down our Main Street. Bands played patriotic songs and groups of veterans and Boy and Girl Scout troops marched. Civic leaders waved from their cars while hundreds gathered on the sidewalks watching the parade

---

[6] Li'l Abner was a sweet-natured male who lived in a fictional clan of hillbillies in Dogpatch, USA, featured in the satirical comic strip created by Al Capp. No one came to our school dressed as skimpily as Daisy Mae, though on Sadie Hawkins Day, gals did run to catch their beaus. Today, the comical fun day would probably be criticized but this popular culture phenomenon made it to the LIFE Magazine cover in 1952.

PONDERING MY JOURNEY

go by. Hands went over hearts whenever the flag passed us. We showed our patriotism. We didn't just give lip service.

Today this holiday, now known as Veterans Day, is not only celebrated in remembrance of the date when World War I ended in Europe but to remember veterans who served in wars that followed.

After the parade, hundreds made their way over to the County Fairgrounds where there was a carnival with amusement rides, booths of games and food, and lots of animals to admire. Finally, going home late at night, we had tummy aches and Kewpie dolls.

Just before graduation, another war about a country named Korea was about to change our lives once again. Guys in our class who turned 18 could sign up for the service of their choice or wait for Uncle Sam to draft them into the Army.

Probably my early school life sounds corny and unsophisticated. But I sometimes reach into these memories to explain to my grandchildren what patriotism was to my generation. And how much it meant to hear the Bible read before we started our class work. And what it was like to see one war end and sad to see another begin.

I am sure you can pull some memories of your growing up years and come up with some fun as well as challenging times in your life to share with some younger people.

Prayer: Lord, I can't change the past, but I can put my memories in the right perspective—letting the good outweigh the not-so-happy ones. So, thank You for all those years! Amen.

Scriptures: "I will give thanks to you, Lord, with all my heart; I will tell of all your wonderful deeds." (Psalm 9:1)

"Do not remember the sins of my youth and my rebellious ways; according to your love remember me, for you, Lord, are good." (Psalm 25:7)

An Unexpected Miracle

At age 16, I had no idea that God's miracle gifts mentioned in the Gospels were still available to Christians. But the Lord had a big surprise for me, though I did not know I would be the recipient of one of His blessings.

That summer after I finished tenth grade, I attended my church's Youth Retreat held at a large beach house sitting right on the sand dunes beside the Gulf of Mexico—about an hour from our home.

On the third day, I was feeling sick and running a fever. Mother came and took me home. Our small town did not have a hospital. The doctor said I had malaria and he ordered quinine for me. But that did not seem to help much. I lay in bed four more days. I guess I went in and out of consciousness, as I did not seem to respond to anyone.

At night after my boyfriend got off from work, he'd come to sit by my bed, always bringing a chocolate milkshake, hoping I would wake up and talk to him. But I never knew he had come.

We lived in the small hotel that my mother managed. She had a great kitchen staff who cooked for our boarders and guests. One day the head "Cook"—we called her that—told Mother about a "Holy Ghost Revival" she was attending at night. She said visiting "faith healers" even prayed for sick people and they were healed.

Since I had not shown improvement, Mother asked her to see if the evangelists holding the meetings would come pray over me.

One afternoon as I lay semi-conscious on my bed in the hotel, I suddenly opened my eyes. A Black man and woman, both dressed in all white clothing, were leaning over me, shouting, "Be healed in Jesus' name! In Jesus' name be healed and get up!" Were they angels? I certainly thought I had died and gone to heaven.

Suddenly I was fully awake. Lying in my bed. Healed. Surprised. Recognizing things around me. They had anointed my head with oil and prayed some Scripture prayers of faith aloud, I later learned.

That night when my boyfriend dropped by, I was sitting in a chair beside the bed. Between sips of that delicious chocolate milkshake, my voice got louder and louder as I tried to explain the details of my miraculous healing.

While my introduction to a miracle healing happened when I was 16, too many years passed before I fully recognized that God still performs wonders and miracles.

Even though I read my Bible over the years, somehow, I missed the truth—perhaps because I was swayed by my church's teaching that miracles ceased after the early church. Later I realized we must build our faith as we meditate on the Word of God. Standing on His promises, speaking His Word, and believing His gifts are for today. They did not all die out with the death of Jesus' disciples.

Years later I attended large healing crusades and saw people miraculously healed. I even went to two packed-out meetings conducted by Kathryn Kuhlman and saw miracles for myself when she prayed for Jesus to touch them. One of my Houston friends attended one of Miss Kuhlman's meetings. At 45, she was given a few weeks to live due to cervical cancer, but Jesus healed her, and she lived another 53 years! She recently stepped into glory just a few weeks shy of 99.

If you have also experienced a miraculous event, or have witnessed one in someone's life, I imagine you aren't bashful about sharing it with others. Telling others builds our own faith as we share that God still moves in supernatural ways even today.

Prayer: Thank You, Lord, that You still heal today! Amen.

Scriptures: "Is anyone among you sick? Let him call for the elders of the church, and let them pray over him, anointing him with oil in the name of the Lord. And the prayer of faith will save the sick, and the Lord will raise him up." (James 5:14-15 NKJV)

"Jesus Christ is the same yesterday and today and forever." (Hebrews 13:8 NKJV)

Prayers from My Youth

In the mornings I said this prayer:

Good morning, God.
This is Your day.
I am Your child.
Show me Your way today. Amen.

At night this prayer:

Now I lay me down to sleep.
I pray the Lord my soul to keep.
If I should die before I wake,
I pray Thee Lord my soul to take.
If I should live another day,
I pray Thee Lord to guide my way.[7]

A Critical Life Change

Looking back at painful times in your life can be uncomfortable. Yet sometimes when you stop to review a few you may recognize once again how God's love, power, and guidance brought you

---

[7] "Now I Lay Me Down to Sleep" was in all likelihood inspired by a very old poem called "The Black Paternoster." Supposedly it was popular in the later Medieval period and ultimately spread to England. The rhyme came to be called "The Four Corners Prayer" and was first published in English by author Thomas Ady in the 1600s, according to Heather Adams. https://www.crosswalk.com/faith/prayer/is-now-i-lay-me-down-to-sleep (Accessed June 23, 2023).

through. Such was my case recently when my sister, my only surviving sibling, visited me and we began to reminisce.

One person's wrong choices can affect many people. My daddy fell in love with his secretary. At Christmas, he put my mother, my small sister, and me on a train in Texas, where we had lived ever since I was a baby, and sent us to live with my mother's sisters in Florida. My two brothers remained with him for a while even after he married his secretary. Daddy later regretted his decision and wanted to remarry Mother. But it was too late. He was still married.

I attended eighth grade in three different towns because of our family's break-up. I lived with one aunt, then the other, while Mother tried to find jobs to help support us. Finally, she relocated in a little town in Northwest Florida named DeFuniak Springs, as manager of her sister Ruth's small hotel. It was more of a boarding house with a large dining room where many locals came for home-cooked meals. Mother got custody of my brothers, so our family seemed more whole.

After I finished two years of high school there, Mother felt I could get a broader education by attending high school in Tallahassee. So, I went to live with her sister Ruth there at her boarding house, the Monroe Inn. I enrolled in a program that placed high school seniors in jobs after they finished their academic classes at noon. I worked for the State of Florida Advertising Department, where we wrote hundreds of letters to help encourage tourists to visit Florida. It sounds ridiculous today when there seems to be an abundance of tourists here now. But that was the way it was in the early 1950s. I kept that job through my college days, except for the summer I worked in Washington, D.C. during the Korean conflict. While attending high school in Tallahassee I traveled with our Spanish class on a field trip to Cuba before it was a communistic country. That first out-of-this-country trip gave me a great desire to someday travel to many nations.

The year I finished high school, Mother made arrangements to buy Aunt Ruth's Monroe Inn in Tallahassee. The Inn usually had forty boarders. The dining room drew an average of 300 or more customers a day—construction workers, college students, even some legislators as it was less than two blocks from the State Capitol. Regular customers enjoyed the homecooked meals, served family-style—heaps of fresh vegetables, hot yeast rolls, tea, and a choice of two meats, all you could eat for 50 cents. Three meals a day, six days a week.

By my college freshman year, my mom took over the Monroe Inn. I enrolled at Florida State University—working two jobs to pay for tuition. Mother thought I should study hotel management, which I did the first year, and I finally said, "No way. I am going to major in something that has to do with writing and communication."

I had started writing Brownie Scout news for our local newspaper as a youngster and I knew writing was hidden deep down in me. So, I switched majors to journalism, and it opened doors for many exciting interviews for newspapers while I was still an FSU student—even one with then Florida Governor Fuller Warren. I had found one of my niches in life with that journalism degree.

Prayer: Father, thank You that even when storms rock our seas, You are there. You get us through. I am so grateful that You never forsake us and that You can bring good out of what seems so bad! Thank You for Jesus, our Savior. And for the Holy Spirit, our Teacher and Comforter. Amen.

Scriptures: "Then they cry out to the Lord in their trouble. And He brings them out of their distresses. He calms the storm so that its waves are still. Then they are glad because they are quiet; So He guides them to their desired haven." (Psalm 107:28-29 NKJV)

"For we are His workmanship, created in Christ Jesus for good works which God prepared beforehand that we should walk in them." (Ephesians 2:10 NKJV)

PONDERING MY JOURNEY

Interruptions During Korean War

In 1951 with the Korean War underway, males who had turned 18 and were scheduled to graduate that spring faced military service. They could enlist in the branch of their choice or be drafted into the Army after graduation. At least that is how I remember it.

Because I had a boy's name, I got two different draft notices. I threw them away. When I did not show up, a military man came to my home to see why I had not responded. After viewing my birth certificate, he was convinced I was not eligible for draft.

But for guys, it was another matter. One Saturday morning I stood on the platform of the train station in DeFuniak Springs with a few other teenagers as we waved off five of the boys from the high school there who were boarding a train to take them to basic training with the U.S. Navy. They had all decided to volunteer to go before they graduated, hoping they could stay together. Amazingly several did later serve on the same ship.

At the time I was a senior at a Tallahassee high school, living with my Aunt Ruth. But DeFuniak Springs, some 125 miles northwest, was where my mom and the rest of my family lived. These boys who enlisted had been my friends and former classmates since we were in the eighth grade, so I went back to see them off.

Then by 1953 when the Korean War was in its third year, and I finished my sophomore year at FSU, five of us gals decided we needed to do our patriotic duty toward the war effort too.

We went to Gainesville, Florida to take a typing test to qualify for military jobs in the Washington D.C. area. All of us passed and were accepted. We learned we could rent rooms at the Young Women's Christian Association (YWCA). The train from Florida to D.C. was so crowded with military men that had not some of them given us their seats and sat in the aisles all night—that's where we girls would have been sitting instead.

Assigned to a Navy job at the Pentagon, I never dared to talk about my duties of tracking ships. Some of my close former classmates were on one of those ships and I knew where they were going but I was careful not to tell them. They wanted letters from home to cheer them up, so we wrote but we also sent them small plastic recordings. We made these by going into small booths similar to a telephone booth, spoke into a machine, and collected the small record that resembled a compact disc to mail them. I often ponder how much easier our jobs would have been had we had desktop computers, or smartphones, or email capacity to do our work or communicate with friends overseas.

My summer was full of exciting new adventures. While I enjoyed my job, I looked forward to weekends because there was so much to see and do in D.C. Sometimes my friends and I rented bikes to ride around the Potomac. Or attended dances at the USO at the nearby Army base —how I loved to dance. One weekend we made it to New York City to see the sights. July 4th was special as we sat on blankets on the lawn at the Washington Mall to listen to the U.S. Marine band play patriotic songs.

That summer Queen Elizabeth was coronated in Westminster Abbey in London. And in D.C. big signs were up everywhere to spare the lives of convicted spies Julius and Ethel Rosenberg.

But then came a Sunday I'll always remember. On July 26, I was sitting in a large church when I noticed someone come in and whisper into the ear of several men sitting in the congregation. I thought I recognized one as a member of the president's cabinet. Each man got up and left the worship service. I suspected something important was happening.

Sure enough the next day, Monday July 27, fighting ended. The Korean War was over.

A few weeks later I returned to Tallahassee, picked up my FSU classes as a junior, and went back to work with the Florida Advertising Department.

PONDERING MY JOURNEY

A new chapter in my life was beginning—though at the time I didn't realize its significance.

Prayer: Lord, thank You for seeing us through uncertain times—for protecting us and for opening doors of opportunities for us to use our skills. We are grateful for those who defend our nation and grateful too when wars end. We thank You for the way You have guided us through our many decisions. Thank You that You have plans for our individual lives and You will help us accomplish them. In the name of Jesus, we pray. Amen.

Scripture: "'For I know the plans and thoughts that I have for you,' says the Lord, 'plans for peace and well-being and not for disaster, to give you a future and a hope. Then you will call on Me and you will come and pray to Me, and I will hear [your voice] and I will listen to you. Then [with a deep longing] you will seek Me and require Me [as a vital necessity] and [you will] find Me when you search for Me with all your heart'." (Jeremiah 29:11-13 AMP)

Part Three: The Adult Years

Meeting a Husband

If you are married, you probably have a fascinating story about how you two met. I hope you have written yours for your descendants to read someday. Here is mine.

She tricked me. My mother tricked me.

"There's the nicest young man among those Florida State guys who come to eat supper here. He's from Texas. I want you to meet him," she told me.

"I do not want to meet a guy from Texas—and you know it. Forget it," I said in a huff as I rushed from the cash register to the dining room to refill glasses of tea for those many hungry men eating at Mom's Monroe Inn boarding house. She had finally raised the price to seventy-five cents for the family-style meals. I continued waiting tables or working as cashier for her every night during my college years.

Texas, that's where I had some bad childhood memories. And as ridiculous as it sounds, I did not want anything to do with a real Texan!

Easter's spring break was coming up and my Army boyfriend, Neal, happened to be temporarily stationed near, of all places, Austin, Texas. He had begged me to come to see him before he was deployed overseas. At Christmas, he had come to Florida to meet my family. Neal, from Ohio, was the special guy I had met at the USO dances at the Army base outside Washington, D.C. while I worked for the Navy.

Mother said I could go meet Neal if she and my Aunt Ruth accompanied me. We could even take her new Buick. I was so excited. It didn't bother me that I was going to have two chaperones. The day arrived. At 5:00 a.m., we got into the car to leave Tallahassee, but Mother drove out to the Florida State campus and stopped at West Hall Men's Dorm. I looked up from the map I was studying while sitting in the back seat and saw a young man with a crew cut slide into our car on the driver's side while Mother scooted over.

"This is LeRoy Sherrer," she said, turning to speak to me in the back seat. "I am sure you have seen him in the college crowd at the Monroe Inn. He lives near Houston so he is going to drive, and we will let him off at the bus station there so he can go on to his hometown." Absolutely shocked at her sly bit of news, I certainly could not raise a fuss because he was already driving us out of town.

Deciding to make the best of our situation, we all had some lively conversation for the next ten or so hours, getting better acquainted and telling funny family stories. He seemed so easy-going and quick to smile. I learned he was on leave from Moody Air Force Base in Valdosta, Georgia under Operation Bootstrap which allowed him to finish his last year of college at FSU. Yet he would have to return to the Air Force base for another year of active duty. I was impressed with the muscles bulging from his short sleeve shirt and even more impressed when he said he had gone to Sam Houston State College on a football scholarship.

Later when we drove into the Houston Greyhound Bus Station, he got out, telling us when he would be there for his return ride back. Mother drove us on to Austin. She, Aunt Ruth, and I shared a hotel room while Neal had one down the hall. He and I had some great walks through the city, and great talks, even discussing the future. He asked me to consider marrying him when he returned to the

States. I did not give him an answer. The Korean War had ended but the U.S. military was still needed in other global hot spots.

I had one and a half wonderful days with Neal, while Mom and my aunt toured the historic sites around Austin. Then it was time to leave. After hugging Neal goodbye, we headed for our first stop: Houston. There LeRoy joined us again as the driver. Both he and my mother suggested I sit up front this time. I did, at first out of curiosity.

But as we got better acquainted, I decided this man, five years older than me, might turn out to be a good friend. But how? He would graduate in only three months, then go back to Moody AFB, about two hours from campus, to finish his military commitment.

"Neal asked me to marry him," I said as we neared the Mississippi border. "Do you think that's a good idea?" I asked while thinking out loud.

"No, definitely not," LeRoy said, reaching over to pat my left hand. I had no idea he had been noticing me when I was waiting tables in Mother's dining room and had wanted to ask me out.

And I didn't marry Neal.

Instead, 21 months later I married LeRoy on Christmas Day after he and I had both finished FSU and he'd completed his Air Force duty. He had put a lot of miles on his old green Pontiac, coming from Georgia to see me in Tallahassee, during his last year in the Air Force.

So, armed with a marriage license, military discharge papers, and $600 between us, we headed for guess where? Texas! He studied for two more years at the University of Houston to earn his mechanical engineering degree. Both of us worked to supplement his G.I. Bill. I was public relations director of a downtown hospital, which required a lot of writing and interaction with the

Houston news outlets. He worked for a centrifugal pump company in the afternoons.

LeRoy wearing his Air Force uniform when he and Quin first met in 1954.

Finally, in 1958 he graduated. His proud parents came for the grand occasion as he was the only one of their children to graduate from college. He had surgery the next day and his football injuries from years earlier continued to plague him a lot during his life.

After he recuperated a while, I drove us back to Florida while he lay in the backseat of our car. He had a new job waiting at the newly established Cape Canaveral Spaceport—an agency related to space flight and aeronautics. He would spend the major part of his career as an aerospace engineer for the National Aeronautics and Space Administration (NASA) at Kennedy Space Center. After arriving in Central Florida, we moved into a mobile home, and I went to work for the Titusville Chamber of Commerce.

Reluctant to meet a Texan? Well, yes, I was, and he did move us back there for short stays. Two of our children were born in Texas, but by then I loved the state almost as much as Florida. But not quite. We were married for nearly 54 years, living out his last days in Florida.

And Neal? He came home to Ohio, settled down, married, and raised a family.

As for meeting and marrying my Texan, I always said my mother was the sneakiest of all matchmakers.

And I was blessed because the man I married encouraged me to use my gifts and talents to write, travel, and lecture on my book topics. He did not hold me back. He once told someone, "If I don't release her to do what God has called her to do, He will get me."

When our children were young, I was able to work at the newspaper office because I had an understanding editor who wanted me as a feature writer. That career allowed me to be home when the kids got out of school in the afternoons as well as some summers.

Have you ever had fun sharing how you met your mate? Once five of us women friends spent a morning over coffee exchanging such stories. What laughter we enjoyed. What warm memories I have of that day.

Quin ready for her wedding on Sunday, Christmas Day 1955.

Just married. Quin's grandfather, Rev. A.M. Moore, officiated at the wedding in the Walton Hotel in DeFuniak Springs, Florida which her Aunt Ruth owned, and which was originally the historic Chautauqua Hotel.

PONDERING MY JOURNEY

Here is a prayer for a husband from our book, *Warfare Prayers for Women*.

Prayer for a Husband

Thank You, Lord, for ___(name)___, the life partner You have given me. Help us to build a strong, happy marriage as we serve You and seek Your blessings upon our family. May we always communicate with one another honestly and lovingly in resolving our differences while giving one another the benefit of the doubt. Thank You for giving him favor with his boss and colleagues at the job. I pray that You will open opportunities for him to advance so that his skills can best be used. Help him to be a good father to our children, assuring them of his unconditional love for them even when discipline is necessary. I stand against any effort by the enemy to bring disunity and division into our family and declare that our home will be a sanctuary where Your presence can dwell. I praise You for this. Amen.[8]

Scriptures: "For this reason, a man will leave his father and mother and be united to his wife, and the two will become one flesh. This is a profound mystery—but I am talking about Christ and the church. However, each one of you also must love his wife as he loves himself, and the wife must respect her husband." (Ephesians 5:31-33)

"Do nothing out of selfish ambition or vain conceit. Rather, in humility value others above yourselves, not looking to your own interests but each of you to the interests of the others." (Philippians 2:3-4)

---

[8] Quin Sherrer and Ruthanne Garlock, *Warfare Prayers for Women*. (Bloomington, MN: Chosen Books, 2020), 122.

Using Our Hands

There are more than 2,000 mentions of the words "hand/hands" in the Bible—no matter what version you read. Here are two I like:

"Let the Lord our God be upon us...and establish the work of our hands for us. Yes, establish the work of our hands" (Psalm 90:17b NKJV)

"Fear not, for I am with you; Be not dismayed, for I am your God. I will strengthen you; Yes, I will help you, I will uphold you with My righteous right hand." (Isaiah 41:10 NKJV)

Think about how many ways you have used your hands during your lifetime. Have you allowed the Lord to use them as His instrument for good? Look at your hands and consider what they have done.

I pondered that question myself recently and then I made a list. Your list will differ greatly from mine since we all have different interests, experiences, and talents.

Looking back over my long life, my "hands list" included:

- Picking cotton with other elementary school students during World War II because the country needed the cotton crop.
- Waiting tables at my mother's Monroe Inn dining room.
- Changing cloth diapers for three babies and hanging them out to dry even in windswept winters—before disposal diapers and affordable clothes dryers were available.
- Housekeeping in a pop-up tent camper with our children while traveling through 25 states to show them our nation's historical and colorful sights from Boston to the Grand Canyon.
- Washing thousands of dishes and cooking hundreds of meals over the years.
- Feeding the dog after the kids left for college.

- Pecking away on numerous keyboards in many locations to write books and articles.
- Covering space launches for the local newspaper near Kennedy Space Center and having the privilege to interview astronauts.
- Shaking hands to greet interesting folks from all walks of life.
- Pulling a red wagon with three small grandchildren on board on our weekly "prayer walk" through my neighborhood.
- Laying hands on people while praying for them—family, friends, or even strangers at retreats.
- Dressing anxiously in a pink hospital gown to undergo 33 radiation treatments following surgery for breast cancer.
- Driving our cars thousands of miles, even towing a U-Haul trailer full of our furniture when moving.
- Using my hands to tend to both my mother and my husband on their deathbeds—a sad task in one way, knowing how much I would miss them—but a joy to know they were going to heaven and be with our Savior, Jesus Christ!
- Holding on to God, He indeed held me by His righteous right hand even in dangerous situations. Like the time when two men appeared at my door early one morning just after my husband left for work asking to use the phone at our home located deep in the woods, far from other houses. Grasping tight to my front door's handle with both hands, I shouted "No!" to them through the door. And I cried out to God for safety and angelic protection. And He answered. (Police later told me I was "lucky" because they were armed, had made a getaway in a stolen car after robbing a convenience store, but got stuck on a dirt road before walking to our house, wanting to call a wrecker.)

Perhaps you will recall the times you knew God was giving you guidance or protection as well. And you too might make a list, then lift it up to the Lord in thanksgiving for the numerous ways you were privileged to use your hands.

Prayer: Father, we are humbled by the many ways You have allowed us to use our hands—for work and fun. Thank You for the people You have brought into our path. We give You praise for being with us during our life's journey. We ask for Your continued blessing on our life. May we be Your hands extended to assist, bless, or love others. In Jesus' name, we ask. Amen.

Scriptures: "I have set the Lord always before me; Because He is at my right hand I shall not be moved." (Psalm 16:8 NKJV)

"Whatever your hand finds to do, do it with all your might." (Ecclesiastes 9:10a NKJV)

"The wise woman builds her house, but the foolish pulls it down with her hands." (Proverbs 14:1 NKJV)

"Do not withhold good from those to whom it is due, when it is in the power of your hand to do so." (Proverbs 3:27 NKJV)

"She extends her hand to the poor. Yes, she reaches out her hands to the needy." (Proverbs 31:20 NKJV)

"Lift up your hands in the sanctuary and bless the Lord." (Psalm 134:2 NJKV)

Part Four: Motherhood Years

Mother to Young Children

Can you remember the days when you had young children and things did not always go smoothly? Or when you enjoyed wonderful adventures? Wait. Maybe you forgot them. I probably would have had I not recorded them in one of two columns I wrote for our local newspaper titled "Good Night, Lord" and "Quin's Quotes and Notes" back in the mid-1960s through 1970s.

Help, Lord—It's Falling Apart

Dear Lord, oh, how I need You. I cannot seem to cope with the problems of modern motherhood. In the span of just one week, I experience these happenings:

A bulldozer clearing the vacant lot behind our house hits the guide wire causing all the various wires leading to our house to come crashing down. What's this? One hot wire, one cold one? For three rain-splattered hours, an endless parade of men stomp through my house and yard. A mere hole in the roof, a bit of an eve chipped off. We'll settle up next week but at least I have electricity throughout the house. Oh Lord, I need You.

I want a pair of shoes for the first grader. The salesman says they're a perfect fit. The kid insists something is sticking him. "Nonsense," says the salesman. "First grade rebellion. Use psychology on him." Instead, he uses psychology on me, and I buy the shoes. On the way home my child yanks off the shoe to show me a nail in the middle of the brand-new shoe. Oh Lord, I need You.

The street is slick from rain, so I cautiously guide the car homeward. Out of nowhere a bug of a car is coming at me—frontwards, now backwards, now sideways, skidding, hitting a parked car ahead of me. I swerve, he misses. Thanks, I needed You, Lord.

Then one night I have a meeting to photograph for my newspaper job. My husband turns down my offer to give the children their baths before I leave. I am the one who usually oversees bath time. But he says tonight he'll do it, thank you very much.

Later, I return home to a humming washing machine and a waltzing clothes dryer. Sheets, towels, and bedspreads are lying helter-skelter all over the garage floor. Good grief, is someone sick or are they all dying?

Moments later I figure out what happened. He let the bath water overflow. See, he went outside to call the youngsters in, but the basketball net and the fresh air were just too inviting. So, he stays a bit too long at play. Like 20 minutes' worth. The carpeted house is flooded. He enlists the aid of neighbors, rents a suction vacuum cleaner, and uses every available piece of linen in the house to soak up water.

He meets me at the door with a sheepish look. "Guess I ruined the carpet," he stammers. I walk squish-squash through the hallway. And I murmur, "Oh, is that all that happened?"

Dear Lord, You know I need You!

The unexpected often happens in a busy, crazy culture, but we can get through when we ask the Lord to help us.

Prayer: Lord, thank You for helping me through difficult days. Amen.

Scripture: "Casting all your care on Him for He cares for you." (I Peter 5:7 NKJV)

Letter to My Last First Grader

Dear Last First Grader: It has become a tradition for me to write each of you children a letter as you begin school.

The other day when I registered you for first grade, I had to fill out a questionnaire that was a real "thinkstopper." It asked me how old you were when you learned to walk and talk. And if you are afraid of the dark. Or if you still suck your thumb or wet the bed.

I couldn't remember without looking at your baby book when you took your first step or uttered your first "Da-Da." At an average age, I'm sure.

Yes, you finally stopped sucking your thumb and wetting your bed. Most kids do eventually. And yes, you've been to a zoo and a museum—in answer to the other questions.

But that cold white sheet of paper didn't leave room to really tell all about you. Like how you caught your first fish before you were three, or how many lengths of a pool you can swim.

It didn't leave room to tell any of your adventures either. That you've toured 25 states in your six young years. That you have skipped down the streets in Boston where Paul Revere once rode to cry his warning. That you've climbed on the replica of the Mayflower at Plymouth Rock and have huffed and puffed up the many steps of United States Capitol in Washington D.C.

That you've stood at quiet attention by the graveside of John F. Kennedy at Arlington National Cemetery and watched in wonder as the eternal torch burned on. You have waved a tiny hand at the big hand holding the torch of freedom—the Statue of Liberty in the harbor of New York.

You have run through the cornfields in Indiana and talked with the Cherokees in North Carolina. You liked Mark Twain's home in Hartford, Connecticut, and were amazed at the Cyclorama reenacting the Battle of Atlanta in Georgia.

You have seen San Antonio's Hemisphere, Arizona's deserts, Florida's caverns. You've witnessed several lift-offs of men into outer space a few miles away from the launchpad while your dad saw it from the control room at the Kennedy Space Center where he's an aerospace engineer.

No place on that form to record that you don't like milk or spinach, but you love spaghetti, chocolate pudding, and peanut butter on crackers. That you sometimes have an independent streak. How you hate those heavy corrective shoes you have to wear to school because you much prefer to run barefoot.

So much I can't record—especially your eagerness to read all the books you can properly devour, even before you start elementary school. My last first grader. I love you very much. Your Mom.

Prayer: Lord, motherhood has been one of the greatest experiences of my life and watching each child develop using his and her talents has been rewarding and inspiring. Thank You for blessing me with this privilege of being a mom. Amen.

Scripture: "All your children shall be taught by the Lord and great will be the peace of your children." (Isaiah 54:13 NKJV)

Out-of-the-Ordinary Days

It's the out-of-the-ordinary experiences that add spice to our days. At least it has for me. Do you have some to share?

It's being disappointed at the ten pesky ducks I helped to raise who are now devouring my garden. But I still love the wild little black duck Jo-Jo and hope he grows up to have better manners.

It's anxiety as I wait for the police to come and kill the sick racoon crouched near our house. Or helping my boy-child nurse the baby owl suffering with a broken wing which he brought to the screen porch to keep until it recovers. And when taking that owl to the vet for real help, I register "Whootie" as its official name.

It's being proud of our Girl Scout who gets the only needlecraft badge in the troop when her mother can't even sew.

It's laughing with delight at the last day of school report card, when it's the little boy who's copped so many A's.

It's letting the kids think they have me fooled sometimes. Like the sweet son who hides his yellow blanket under his bed each morning after he makes his bed, just so he won't have to fold it neatly. Doesn't he know mothers clean sometimes? Or the ten-year-old who jumps up from the supper table to run and practice her piano. She's not really getting out of doing the dishes. They'll wait for her.

It's taking our first trial run at camping and discovering we brought all the wrong things.

It's going to an out-of-town convention with my husband—minus the kids.

Of course, each day brings a unique and sometimes challenging circumstance—giving us cause to laugh or cry. The better we bounce during the unexpected, the more we can know contentment.

Prayer: Lord, help me laugh more often at what comes my way even on not-so-ordinary days. I know laughter is good for my health, and You told us to be joyful. Amen.

Scripture: "He will fill your mouth with laughter and your lips with shouts of joy." (Job 8:21)

Talking Toys

It's absolutely fun to recall some days when your kids were youngsters and laugh as you share them with your children's children. I hope you have had that happy experience too.

PONDERING MY JOURNEY

This came from my newspaper column, "Quin's Quotes 'N Notes" in the mid-1960s:

When the wee one in our household joined the pre-school set, it gave me Tuesday and Thursday mornings free for house cleaning and desk work.

While the three-year-old wanted to go to school very much, the first day she acted apprehensive. "Who will take care of you while I'm gone, Mother?" she asked. "Won't you get lonesome?"

I didn't have an answer—not until I had cleaned house. Then I found out that in this house I would never get lonely.

I started in her room first, hoping to discard some very tattered junk. The vacuum bumped the toy box and out walked Pinocchio. He walked swiftly just like a wooden boy carved in Geppetto's workshop should walk. He had been left wound up tight, so he walked right over to me.

I almost laughed aloud until the vacuum knocked into the doll cradle. I was not prepared for this surprise. Terry, the talking doll, said loud and clear, "Let's play school." Terry is like that. She will talk at the least bump. It doesn't need someone to push her button for her to start talking. Just like her owner. Those chatty ones deserve each other.

In the boy-child's room I met an animal who said, "Isn't it silly talking to a horse?" And while it was, I said, "Hello" to Mr. Ed. He replied to me, "The phone is ringing. Shall I answer it?" That was too much.

I would've gone batty with only the company of Mr. Ed in the son's room, so while I dusted I half-listened to "Jack and the Beanstalk" on the Show-and-Tell machine. Better plot than *Dragnet*.

The other daughter's room was last. Chatty Cathy eyed me suspiciously from her bed. It takes a lot of coaxing to make that doll talk, but just for kicks, I pulled her string. "Will you play with me?" she begged. Sounded familiar.

By now I was glad Penny, Heidi, Jan, and the others did not have voice boxes. I'd never get my work done.

When the nursery schoolgirl returned home, I told her about my morning's adventure in Toyland.

"I will never get lonesome with so many little people hiding in corners and cradles and toy boxes," I assured her.

No, I will do just fine as long as I can remember not to answer them back or tell them to catch the phone.

Prayer: Heavenly Father, thank You for days when we can laugh at things that happened in our home—even years later. I am grateful for the family You gave me. And I am also glad we are part of Your family! Amen.

Scripture: "Then our mouth was filled with laughter, and our tongue with singing; then they said among the heathen, the Lord hath done great things for them." (Psalm 126: 2 KJV)

Get Out of His Way

Every house needs at least one little boy. That's what I've been preaching for the past six years since one joined our household.

He has enriched our lives, broadened our experiences, challenged our patience, and made us sometimes question our wisdom.

At an early age, little girls begin pretending they are mothers. They have baby dolls and miniature stoves. They borrow mother's old high heels and timeworn hats. They tie frilly aprons over long skirts.

Chances are, when they are grown, they will be surrounded with real life dolls who squirm and cry and get sick. And they will have their own shiny stoves and high heels and felt hats and gingham aprons.

But take the plight of a male. He will probably settle on one occupation. It may be dull, boring, unchallenging. Or it could be exciting, promising, fulfilling.

But when he is still a little boy, he can lapse into the world of make-believe and disappear into any role that strikes his fancy fantasy.

Unlike the little girl who borrows mother's cast-off clothes, this little boy must have an array of costumes to enact his roles.

One morning he dons a cape and a fierce-looking hat that covers part of his face. He announces that for the moment he's Batman. Clear out of his way! He wants to leap from the top of his six-foot-high fort. But instead, he ties ropes on the roof, so Batman can swing easily through the air.

Minutes later he's wearing a headdress of sweeping colored feathers and a beaded buckskin suit. He pauses to shoot arrows into the air because he's Chief Rainwater. Out of his way!

Almost as quickly he decides that being a cowboy would be more fun. Should he wear his Davy Crockett coonskin cap or the Western ten-gallon hat? Now where did he leave his boots? Out of his way!

But soon this play grows stale. He's now inspired to become G.I. Joe—knapsack, canteen, compass, and camouflaged helmet. Out of his way! When the water and crackers give out and the little boy tires of crawling on his belly in the tall grass out behind the house, he switches costumes once more.

Now he is an astronaut. His silver-gray spacesuit comes equipped with two zippers and his helmet is a copy of the original. He makes himself a rocket out of a tall cardboard box. When he can't launch himself, he hollers for mother. As soon as she announces the countdown and helps him blast off, he shouts, "Out of my way!" And he's off on an adventure in space that could occupy his time for at least 30 minutes.

Then Daddy comes home from work. The little boy runs for the football, protective helmet, and sweatshirt with his favorite number on it. Already he fancies himself as a college football player like his daddy was. He kicks the ball and runs for a 40-yard dash. A powerhouse is loose. Out of his way!

Not once has he imagined himself an engineer, or schoolteacher, or salesman. His make-believe world is charged with high adventure.

One day he's bound to grow tired of swinging from ropes or bursting out of a cardboard rocket.

But for now, at bedtime, when Mother tucks in her Batman-cowboy-soldier-football star, she's also requested to cover up the fat brown teddy bear who still sleeps with him.

And then they say their prayers.

A family blessed with a son is up for heaps of surprises, lots of laughs, and thousands of wonderful, happy adventures.

Prayer: Lord, thank You so much for this son who has brought such joy to us. Help him as he matures to become the man You planned for him from his birth. Help us be the parents he needs to help guide him on his path. Amen.

Scripture: "'For I know the plans I have for you,' declares the Lord, 'plans to prosper you and not to harm you, plans to give you hope and a future.'" (Jeremiah 29:11)

My Hope with His Frog

Dear First Grade Teacher,

Rest well this summer, dear teacher. Come fall I will send you one blue-eyed lad, quite small for his age, who is already weaving big dreams.

Sometimes he says he doesn't want to grow up, for he's heard that grown up boys often go to war—like his dad had to. He loves life too much.

PONDERING MY JOURNEY

He also likes chocolate ice cream, raw carrots, electric trains, guitars, animals, and the boastful boy on the next block.

He hates to brush his teeth, eat cooked vegetables, put on his shoes, or discard his junk. He collects mix-matched cards, seashells, rocks, bird feathers, and records with a Hawaiian beat.

"Wait a minute," is his most-used expression. He knows his ABCs and the necessary numbers. "Why, that's kid stuff," he brags to his baby sister.

He's heard tales about school principals, school bus drivers, and lunchroom proctors from the older and wiser boys who have already traveled the first grade path. Frankly, he's a bit frightened.

He comes to you with a great deal of curiosity, a vivid imagination, and an oversupply of enthusiasm.

He is presently shy but very eager to please. If you will just "wait a minute."

You will be the first scholarly link to an outside and foreign world. As you help him sort and accumulate his lessons, I trust you will do it with patience, understanding, and a bit of humor.

I realize he will be only one of more than 30 in your room—a real challenge for you, no doubt. But you see, he's not just a number or face to me.

He's my boy, with all his faults and complexes and needs. He's my hope for the future. And whether he wants to or not, he will grow up to be some other gal's hope too.

Someone once said, "A boy is the hope of the future with a frog in his pocket."

I send you, dear teacher, my hope along with his frog.

From the boy's mother.

Prayer: Lord, as I send this child off to his new world of school, I ask for Your watchcare over him, his friends, and his teachers both now and throughout his school years. Lord, may he, like Daniel, show aptitude for every kind of learning, be well informed, quick to understand. May he have a keen mind and knowledge and understanding and the ability to solve difficult problems. Give him wisdom and great insight and a breadth of understanding as measureless as the sand on the seashore. Thank You. Amen. (Daniel 1:4; 2:14; 5:12; I Kings 4:29)

Scripture: "Blessed [fortunate, prosperous, and favored by God] is the man who does not walk in the counsel of the wicked [following their advice and example], Nor stand in the path of sinners, Nor sit [down to rest] in the seat of scoffers (ridiculers). But his delight is in the law of the Lord, And on His law [His precepts and teachings] he [habitually] meditates day and night." (Psalm 1:1-2 AMP)

Quin took this photo of their family camping out with church friends as they gathered for Sunday morning worship services.

Hoping My Children Remember

As my children grow up, I hope they will remember about our home that:

PONDERING MY JOURNEY

God comes first.

Their mother and daddy love each other.

Each child has both a talent and a personality of his or her own to develop to the fullest.

Health is to be treasured above wealth.

Hard work is a virtue, not a curse.

Friendship is one of the greatest gifts of life, especially those that withstand the tidal waves of years.

Sunday is the happiest day of the week: the day our family worships together and later plays together.

Praying is a natural, everyday thing, and not just a "sometime" anchor to grab when life seems to be tossing you wildly about.

You must reserve time for yourself each day to be alone in quiet thoughts.

Minds are made to inquire, explore, and use to the best of your ability for good.

Books can open fascinating doors forever, and no book on our shelves is off base for inquiring young minds.

Camping is one of those family fun times when we can recharge physical and spiritual batteries and find a comforting sense of intimacy with God and each other by enjoying His outdoors.

Traveling is an education in itself, and we return from each adventure more keyed up about life and the world around us.

It can be a beautiful experience to recognize and celebrate the uniqueness of other people.

Because we are human, home will never be perfect. Nor will life. Brothers and sisters often disagree. But deep down there is a common bond drawing our family together.

It's simply LOVE. I hope our children never forget that little four-letter word.

L-O-V-E.

Prayer: Lord, I pray my children will always put God first place in their lives and that each will find ways to express love to one another.

Scripture: "Love is patient, love is kind. It does not envy, it does not boast, it is not proud. It is not rude, it is not self-seeking, it is not easily angered, it keeps no record of wrongs. Love does not delight in evil but rejoices with the truth. It always protects, always trusts, always hopes, always perseveres." (1 Corinthians 13: 4-7)

Their Grandmother's Legacy of Love

"Live the legacy you want to leave because legacy lives on in people, and people live on after you are gone," John C. Maxwell wrote. Oh, how true. Think about the legacy of grandmothers. My children still miss my mom, Mama Jewett, and her prayers and expressions of love.

When they were young, my mom had some small rental cottages named Silver Sands, on the harbor in the fishing village of Destin, Florida. Over their growing up years my three children loved to visit her there.

They could dive off her dock or swim across to Holiday Island or go with her to the nearby Gulf of Mexico for a romp in the waves. They collected seashells and cooked crabs and went fishing in the little pools all around her place.

She would sing with them, read to them, let them sit up late, and study the stars. She'd even recite the "elocution" pieces she learned as a girl in high school—poetry and long essays she still remembered from the 1920s.

PONDERING MY JOURNEY

But it wasn't all play. When work was involved, she made it fun, too, working alongside them. Over the years they learned how to book reservations for the cottages over the phone, how to rent them out, and how to help her clean them after the guests checked out.

Quin's mom, Jewett, at her Silver Sands Cottages on the harbor in Destin, Florida, where the town's billboard reads: "The World's Luckiest Fishing Village."

She taught my children safety rules, expected obedience when she spoke and rewarded them with privileges. Grandchildren were to be enjoyed and loved, she said. When they came back home, they talked nonstop about their adventures and admitted they shared some special secrets with her.

As they grew older, they called her for prayer whenever they were facing a hard time—a dreaded exam in college, a financial setback, a broken relationship—and she would pray for them right then on the phone. Sometimes she even tucked a bit of money in a handwritten letter to them, full of encouragement, cheering them on.

Often in her devotional times of prayer, she would raise her hands to heaven and say, "Lord, these ten fingers represent my ten grandchildren. Now I bring them before You and Your throne to pray for them." And she would pray specifically for each one.

Quin's mother, known as "Mother Jett" to her 10 grandchildren.

She died just a few weeks before our son graduated from Florida State University. As our family gathered on the lawn after the graduation ceremony, we glanced across the Tallahassee skyline—where Mom once had a boarding house—and we began to reminisce about her.

"Oh, how I wish Mother Jewett could be with us here today," our youngest said.[9]

Yes, we missed her terribly—she who had bestowed so much love and prayers into her grandchildren, and into all of us really. Leaving us a rich legacy in memories.

Just the other day when Mom's second great-great grandson was born, his uncle called asking me for a story about her to put in the scrapbook he was making for the newest in Mom's extending family. What fun I had talking about her adventures.

I am sure you too have some happy memories of grandmothers you have known—who have enriched your life and taught you lessons you never forgot. May each of us determine to leave a lasting legacy to our children's children, one that will continue for generations to come. A legacy of love, spiritual influence, and prayer.

Prayer: Thank You, God, for grandmothers who bless so many lives as they invest time, love, and prayers into the lives of their grandchildren. Amen.

Scripture: "For I am mindful of the sincere faith within you, which first dwelled in your grandmother Lois and your mother Eunice, and I am sure that it is in you as well." (2 Timothy 1:5 NASB)

Becoming a Grandmother, Myself

I got word of the birth of my first grandchild, born on the island of Kona, Hawaii, while I was speaking at a Christian retreat center in the mountains of Pennsylvania. When my prayer partner, Jane, went to get us early morning coffee, the hotel clerk told her that during the night a message had come to tell me that a baby girl had been born.

---

[9] Quin Sherrer, *Grandma, I Need Your Prayers.* (Grand Rapids, MI: Zondervan, 2002), 61.

"You're a grandmother! A grandmother! A grandmother!" Jane shouted excitedly while I did a happy dance across the room.

A grandmother. It was hard for me to comprehend the new title tacked onto my name. A new identity. I had wondered at times whether I'd ever be a grandmother. No need to worry. Six years after my first grandchild, I had six—three girls and three boys! Three were born overseas.

Quin with her mother, Jewett Moore, in the 1970s.

After my children moved to where we lived in Colorado, our house was soon filled with paraphernalia that goes with tending to babies and toddlers. Highchairs, baby beds, potty chairs. Children's books, toys, games, puzzles, kid videos, and music tapes. Our fenced yard now had a swing set, T-ball stands, and a miniature basketball court.

If you dropped by our house, you would probably find me sitting on the floor with two or three grandchildren building railroad stations out of plastic blocks, or drinking imaginary tea from tiny china cups, or sitting in a sandbox making sandcastles. I'd be wearing my favorite sweatshirt that says, "Grandmas Are Antique Little Girls."

When they come to my house, I try to stop whatever I'm doing to give them attention. When they stay overnight, we have the best time playing and praying. They are among the most important people in my life whom I can influence for God's purposes.

On my stairway I have a "grandmother wall" containing photos of the grands, and in the middle is a framed poster a daughter gave me with these words:

> Grandchildren bring sunshine into my heart,
> And laughter into my household.
> Their visits may be long or short, but always memorable.
> I tell them my stories and they tell me theirs right back.
> It's my grandchildren that actually make me a grandparent,
> So, I am eternally grateful.
> They always bring such spirited joy into my life.
> —Author unknown

I had the privilege to co-author *Grandma, I Need Your Prayers* with Ruthanne Garlock. Then I wrote on my own *Prayers from a Grandma's Heart* and a journal for grandmothers to record their own prayers titled *Grandma's Prayers*.

Prayer: Dear Lord, thank You for blessing me with grandchildren. Show me ways to bless them, encourage them, and be available for them. Please reveal to me when and how to pray for their spiritual, physical, and emotional well-being. I want to be a godly grandparent they can emulate; thank You for equipping me to do this. Amen.

Scriptures: "One generation will commend your works to another; and they will tell of your mighty acts." (Psalm 145:4)

"I have not stopped giving thanks for you, remembering you in my prayers. I keep asking that the God of our Lord Jesus Christ, the glorious Father, may give you the spirit of wisdom and revelation, so that you may know him better. I pray also that the eyes of your heart may be enlightened in order that you may know the hope to which he has called you." (Ephesians 1:16-18)

From the Mouths of Grandchildren

If you are a parent or grandparent, I'm sure you too have learned some valuable lessons from the mouths of the children in your life. They can utter the most amazing comments that speak to our heart. Priceless keepsakes to store in our memory bank. How we thank God for His gift of children—whom Jesus treasures too.

About midmorning I heard a light knock at my door and went to answer. "Home? Home? Anyone home?" my 20-month-old grandson Lyden Benjamin asked, a big grin on his face.

I was home that Sunday morning because I had attended Saturday night church services—not something I did regularly.

I was startled to see him standing there. He had run away from his own home. He knew his grandmother's arms would be waiting, and he was lonesome for me.

Safe. Sound. Secure. Food. Fun. Hugs. Cheers.

But he had crossed the street alone, and it concerned me. How glad I was that I was home to hold him and call his mom to report that I had her run-away child.

Once when he was a bit older, I had just gotten home from a weeklong speaking engagement when his mom dropped him off at our house. He followed me from room to room while I unpacked and headed to the utility room to wash my dirty clothes. Suddenly I felt Lyden Benjamin's little hand tug on my skirt, trying to grab my undivided attention.

"Sit down, Mama Quin. I've come to keep you company," he said in a boisterous plea.

We plopped down on the blue couch in the den, and he snuggled under my arm, while we watched his favorite "Veggie Tales" video. Then I read to him from some *Thomas the Train* books. Clothes could be washed another time. Unpacking could wait. This child—my precious grandchild—had come to keep me company!

Another time when he overheard my husband caution me to be safety minded when I was about to leave on a speaking trip to the New York area—Manhattan, Brooklyn, Queens, Harlem—this young grandson grabbed my hand and offered a powerful, one-sentence prayer for me. "Dear God, don't let Mama Quin get mugged and let her preach real good. Amen."

One Christmastime, five of my young grandchildren were helping me decorate. They had put together the olive wood nativity set—the creche—but the figure representing the baby Jesus was lost somewhere among the decorations. They searched for some time but could not find the tiny missing baby.

Three-year old Samuel went throughout the house calling out, "Jesus, where are you? Come back to our house. Come back to our house to stay." His words echoed in my heart throughout that Christmas season. A child had pleaded what was important to him and to me. "Come. Come stay."[10]

When Victoria Jewett was seven days old, we had a service in our home to dedicate her to the Lord. Family members joined her parents, Quinett and Michael, as we read Scripture and prayed

---

[10] Selections from my book *Prayers from a Grandma's Heart*. (Grand Rapids, MI: Zondervan Inspirio, 2002).

God's blessing and protection for our newest little bundle of joy. I thought about that special occasion two years later when she was in the hospital, very ill with pneumonia. I cried out to God day and night for her life. One day after she was home, she stomped her little foot and announced, "My name is Victoria Jewett. Don't call me Sissy or Tori." Everybody got the message.

Framed on My Grandmother Wall of Photos

"One hundred years from now it will not matter what your bank account held, the sort of home you lived in, or the kind of car you drove. But the world may be a different place because you were important in the life of a child." (Author unknown).

Prayer: Father God, thank You for sending Your Son, Jesus Christ to live and die for us, and for sending the Holy Spirit to guide and help us now that Jesus is in heaven with You. Thank You too for our little ones who can talk to You with such faith and hope. Help me as a follower of Jesus Christ be a good example to them. I pray in His name. Amen.

Scripture: "Behold, children are a heritage from the LORD. The fruit of the womb is a reward... Yes, may you see your children's children." (Psalm 127:3; 128:6 NKJV)

An Ode to a Garage

A garage is a building for housing automobiles.

However, most garages hold anything but the family wheels.

They shelter bicycles and boats. Washing machines and Dad's old coats.

Trikes, wagons, and skates. Tracks and tunnels for electric trains.

Woodshop benches and hammers and saws. Guinea pigs, plus cats or dogs.

They are home for bridge tables and lawn chairs. Storm windows and portable stairs.

PONDERING MY JOURNEY

They hold this and that and all the other. And oh, yes, the hurricane shutters.

There are boxes and boxes of heavens knows what. Now where did we pack that machine? I have corn to pop.

There are scrapbooks and textbooks, catalogues, and magazines. Pictures and postcards and most anything!

There are trunks and lamps and mops and brooms. Some yellowed newspapers and some rusty old spoons.

There are two lawnmowers, a rake, and a hoe. A broken fan and a TV that won't glow.

A chair that needs upholstering and a desk that needs paint. A straw hat from Mexico and some seashells that stink.

I know a garage that is full, full, full. Please, nothing more, I politely think.

Then the husband comes home with 1,245 light bulbs to add. His civic club is selling; he's sure the community will buy.

In the meantime, I just sit down to cry.

Prayer: Lord, I know we need to unclutter and also become better stewards of material things. Forgive us for hoarding and not sharing what we could give to others who have a need. Amen.

Scripture: "There is a time to keep and a time to throw away." (Ecclesiastes 3:6)

Part Five: Influencers

Purposefully Influencing for Good

When I read that sociologists say we will influence or be influenced by 10,000 people in our lifetime, I found it hard to believe.[11] What do you think?

Well, I changed my mind after I gave serious thought about all the people who do influence us. Think about it. Relatives, friends, teachers, preachers, neighbors, doctors, nurses, politicians, bosses, co-workers, salespersons, repairmen, waitresses, policemen, realtors, bankers, office clerks, and many more.

In turn, we have our own sphere of influence. People whose lives we touch. Some we are aware of, others we are not. So, it could amount to 10,000 in our lifetime.

Influencing is "the power to change or affect someone or something; to cause changes without directly forcing them to happen." So, we can choose to influence for good, not bad; to help, not hurt; to serve, not abuse; to encourage, not discourage. "Live purposefully and worthily," the Apostle Paul advised.

Jamie Buckingham, in writing to Christians, said: "Most of us don't realize it, but our influence is much larger than we can imagine—and will continue for generations to come, be it good or evil. It's a wonderful responsibility. Always remember though,

---

[11] John C. Maxwell, *Developing the Leader Within You*, Thomas Nelson Publishers, Nashville, TN, 1993, 2.

PONDERING MY JOURNEY

Jesus is ever with you and His Spirit will whisper just the things you need to say and do."[12]

Maybe you would like to jot down ways other people or things have influenced and blessed you. Then recall ways you were a helpful influencer. Let's thank God for those priceless occasions! Questions to consider:

- Who were the people you let influence you? Mentor, encourage, correct, advise, or teach you something? What lessons did you learn? What lasting words of encouragement do you cherish? Did you thank them?
- Who were those you influenced on purpose? You spoke into their life. Or helped them develop a skill. Or you just enjoyed sharing food, fun, and fellowship. But you invested time with them.
- Who were those you never knew but whose acts or achievements greatly influenced you?
- Who were the somebodies who wrote a book, painted a picture, composed music, taught you a lesson, preached a sermon, or did something so impressive you were profoundly touched? Do you have some heroes of faith? Why not share their stories?[13]

Prayer: Father, bless those who have made a helpful and significant influence on me. Amen.

Scripture: "Look carefully then how you walk! Live purposefully and worthily and accurately, not as the unwise and witless, but as wise (sensible, intelligent people), making the very most of the time." (Ephesians 5:15, 16a AMPC)

---

[12] Jamie Buckingham, *The Nazarene*. (Ann Arbor, MI: Servant Publications, 1991), 89.
[13] Quin Sherrer, *Cast Your Shadow: Influence on Purpose*. (Kindle, 2018), 199.

Be a Participant in Life

Four pastors stand out as some of the greatest influencers in my life. Not only did they help me grow in my spiritual life, but each in his own way encouraged and supported me to use my God-given giftings in practical ways.

Those pastors were Jamie Buckingham, Peter Lord, Forrest Mobley, and Dutch Sheets. Three of them are now in heaven. I thank God for sending each into my life.

"A good writer needs to be a participant in life—not just a spectator." My writing mentor, Jamie Buckingham, author of dozens of best-selling books, gave me that advice as he edited my magazine article with his red pen while we sat on my living room couch one October evening in early 1974 in Titusville, Florida.

He had been one of my instructors when I won Guideposts Writers Workshop contest a year earlier and had agreed to continue to coach me after it ended since we lived less than an hour apart in Florida.

"Watch people—how they act and react, how they think and reach conclusions. See what makes them tick. The Christian writer's words are his tools, and those tools should constantly be proclaiming the message of the living Christ. Think communication. Writers must be extremely disciplined," he said.

He added, "Every once in a while, I will sit down and write in one sentence what I feel my purpose in life is. I feel my mandate is to impart the Holy Spirit to the generation in which I live. Basically, God's been saying the same thing over the past several years to me."

I was a journalist for our local newspaper and a freelance writer for various magazines. To participate in life rather than just be a spectator was advice I wanted to heed. So, over the next few years I took his counsel.

PONDERING MY JOURNEY

Jamie Buckingham, Quin's writing mentor, at his computer. He eventually wrote 47 Christian-themed books, many bestsellers.

As a parent, I got involved in school board meetings and used my newspaper stories to push for some causes. The mayor gave me "The Outstanding Young Woman Award" for my civic participation one year. I got to know a few moms with special needs children and spent some mornings helping give a ten-year-old her required physical exercises. And I was in the search party with the deputies the day she ran away from home. Hours later she was found safe.

I asked to be locked in jail one day to get the feeling of an inmate. I scrubbed up to watch a surgery in an operating room. I researched carefully before I interviewed a returning astronaut. I interviewed a man running for president of the United States.

With my press pass, camera, and notepad, I got acquainted with schoolteachers, principals, and students and sat in on classes to write their stories. I got to know hospital workers, politicians, doctors, lawyers, engineers, and retail employees. They had fascinating stories which they were glad for me to write and publish.

Jamie Buckingham not only served as pastor of the Tabernacle Church in Melbourne, Florida, he travelled to villages and outposts throughout the world to spend time with those whose stories he would write about. Wycliffe Bible translators at their remote jungle posts. Nomads in the deserts of the Middle East. Into the Holy Land and into the wilderness of the Sinai numerous times, tracing the journey of the children of Israel and writing about contemporary life there.

For his first book, *Run, Baby, Run* for Nicky Cruz, Jamie travelled with Nicky to his old hangouts in Brooklyn, where he was once a street gang warlord, to try to get a feel what his life was like before Jesus changed him. Jamie wrote 12 books for Katherine Kuhlman, capturing the healing testimonies of hundreds who were healed by God's touch during her meetings. He penned one book, *Tramp for the Lord*, for Corrie ten Boom, a survivor of the Holocaust, who became a world-wide travelling evangelist. By his late 50s, Jamie had written 47 books—with 34 million copies sold—many bestsellers among Christian readers.

He had faith in me and time for me. Always pushing me on: "Be a participant in life—and go write how Jesus changes lives." I tried. I went on to write or co-author a number of Christian books—many translated into foreign languages.

The last time I saw Jamie we were both autographing books for the same publisher at the Christian Booksellers Association convention. With his wife Jackie beside him, he said with a teasing smile, "We've come a long way, Quin." Yes, we had. The next year (1992) just before his 60th birthday, he left for heaven.

I could never fully express my gratitude for what his life and advice meant to me. But my joy now is to share with others what he shared with me. So, to hopeful writers, I say, "Go participate in life. And write about it. Someone somewhere will read it and be blessed. And you as the writer/communicator will hear God's whisper of thanks for using your talent wisely."

Quin's writing mentor, Rev. Jamie Buckingham, and Rev. Forrest Mobley, her spiritual mentor, Episcopal priest and friend, met when Quin introduced them in the mid-1970s. Some framed book covers of Jamie's 47 books are on the wall in the Buckingham home.

Prayer: Thank You, Lord, for all the encouragers in our life. May we in turn encourage others too. Thank You for the excellent examples that Jesus gave us as we study the Gospels and read how He went about doing good. Amen.

Scripture: "Therefore encourage one another and build each other up, just as in fact you are doing." (1 Thessalonians 5:11)

Tribute to Pastor Peter Lord

"Welcome to the Lord's House," read the sign outside the home of Rev. Peter Lord and his wife, Johnnie. Not long ago, he got a similar greeting in heaven, "Welcome to the Lord's house." But this time it was Jesus Himself welcoming the 91-year-old beloved pastor emeritus of Park Avenue Baptist Church in Titusville, Florida to heaven.

Last time I visited him he was 86, a widower, and still teaching another generation of people three times a week in his home. Back in the 1970s he was our pastor. I was a mom of three teens, and a newspaper reporter, and my husband was a NASA engineer, when Peter Lord taught us practical ways to live out our Christian faith.

How We Met

One Sunday morning at seven o'clock, I was kneeling at the coffee table in my living room asking God to use me in more ways. The phone rang. It was Peter Lord asking me to give my testimony in his Baptist church that night. Wow, that was an answer to my prayer in a hurry.

I didn't know him personally, but he had written a letter to my newspaper editor thanking him for the articles I was writing.

After I had a spiritual experience—encountering the Holy Spirit in a new way—while attending an Episcopal Church in the Florida Panhandle that summer of 1972, I had returned home with a greater hunger to tell others about our Lord Jesus. When I asked my Star Advocate newspaper editor, Bob Hudson, to let me write a "Fortress of Faith" feature each Friday, he gave me the go-ahead. I'd interview a local pastor, then write about him and his church's history, with pictures to illustrate. For that full page I also interviewed businessmen and women who told me how their faith had helped them through life.

I was somewhat intimidated that night, speaking for Peter Lord's large church. But I did tell the congregation that I had recently made Jesus my Lord, though He had been my Savior since I was a child.

My husband and I continued to attend our denominational church, yet we grieved over changes made in our teaching materials. Finally, after much prayer and counsel from Christian leaders we trusted, we knew it was time for a church change.

So, we invited Pastor Lord to come to our house and talk to us. He answered our questions, and we answered his. We believed we had found a new church home that was the right "fit" for our family. In looking back, I can see how much we benefitted by studying the Bible under a pastor who was so well grounded in the Word of God.

Not long after we joined his church, Peter Lord came back to ask if he could disciple a group from the church in our home on Sunday nights after the five o'clock service ended. We said yes.

So, for the next six years, he taught seven couples in our home on Sunday nights from seven to nine o'clock. I usually served the group a light supper. Then on Wednesday nights in our living room, my husband and I shared with 14 more people the Biblical principles Pastor Lord had taught us. We drank deeply from the well of Peter Lord's experiences with the Living Lord those Sunday evenings when our living room seemed like a holy sanctuary as he taught us in his Jamaican accent. We did that until our family moved.

He called them "discipleship groups" but today we'd call it mentoring in spiritual and practical ways. Pastor Lord had groups like ours scattered all over the town that met on Sunday and Wednesday nights in homes.

Once he spent the whole year teaching us about the "one another" Scriptures from the New Testament. He explained that "reciprocal living" involves one anothers who will pray, serve, encourage, forgive, love, comfort, bear burdens for one another. Biblical commands are both direct and indirect and specify how Christians are to relate to others.

Rev. Peter Lord, pastor of Park Avenue Baptist Church in Titusville, Florida, author of a popular book on prayer, taught seven couples in Quin's home for six years on Sunday nights during the late 1970s.

Pastor Lord asked church members who were willing to volunteer their talents to help one another to register their name and talent at the church office. Then those who needed help in some area could call for help. Some who taught included: Margaret, bread baking. LeRoy, to repair cars. Larry, how to fish with results. Quin, writing classes. Liz, flower arranging. Gene, carpentry skills. Dot, sewing lessons. Youth members did yard work for the elderly. Lib babysat for young moms. Jim flew the pastor on mission trips (my husband was the extra pilot). These and many more were busy for years sharing their giftings with one another. I wrote a series of four booklets on prayer and hospitality, each 40 pages long, which Peter published for the church women.

PONDERING MY JOURNEY

Mary Jo gathered a team of church women and decorated homes in the community every Thursday—all free of charge. Years later we counted up the results and realized that 60 women had participated in her "Ministry of Helps" by decorating over 1,000 homes. Peter had let her redo his office and home first to prove to us he trusted this ordinary homemaker who learned how to manage well during the Great Depression.

If you were invited to eat Sunday dinner at Peter and Johnnie Lord's table, he would ask you, "What has Jesus done for you this week?" Guests would then be expected to relate what wonderful things we had seen Him do. That was the entire table talk—about Jesus working in our everyday lives.

When he wanted to teach us how to conduct family devotions, he demonstrated with his family, including his five children. Their den furniture was moved to the church stage and the kids, wearing their pajamas, sat where they usually did. Then they all participated in their usual 30-minute family devotional routine, with Bible reading and prayer. Now, we in the congregation had no excuse for not duplicating something similar in our homes. But he had a sense of humor too and did all kinds of unusual things to demonstrate a sermon.

While teaching us in 1976, he wrote a prayer journal *The 2959 Plan: A Guide to Communion with God* (2959 means almost 30 minutes). It soon became popular throughout the nation. I once met a pastor in Kentucky who said praying the way Peter taught in that book helped him get through seminary.

To make visitors feel welcome and to encourage us to be hospitable, Pastor Lord asked visitors to stand up in church at the end of the Sunday morning service. Then he asked, "Who is taking them home to eat at your table today? Go find a family." At least two Sundays a month, my husband and I did that. It was not unusual to have a dozen around our dining table for a meal which I prepared mostly on Saturday. (Once a month my teenagers invited their friends for lunch.)

Pastor Lord instigated the church's new Retreat Center where numerous Christian groups came for teaching and refreshing. He also urged church members to go to the Prayer Chapel at least once a week to pray. Nothing else was allowed there—no weddings or other celebrations. Just prayer!

I can't even imagine what all Peter Lord is doing in his new life in heaven now. Many are there enjoying eternity because of him. He had such a passion for winning souls. I keep a picture of the two of us together on my prayer board. Just seems too soon to remove his smiling face.

I am forever grateful to Peter Lord and the other pastors who have invested in my life over the years. I am sure you too have some you want to thank God for because of their contribution to your Christian growth. Pastors not only set great examples by living Christ-centered lives, they inspire hundreds to follow Jesus and to use their talents and experience to help others.

Prayer: Lord, thank You for the pastors who have taught and discipled us. Help us to be faithful to pass along what we learned. Let us truly remember Your commands of all the one anothers as we extend our hands and heart to help others. In Jesus' name. Amen.

Scripture: "God has given each of you some special abilities; be sure to use them to help each other, passing onto others God's many kinds of blessings." (1 Peter 4:10 TLB)

Wear Your Own Shoes

Have you ever wished you could walk in someone else's shoes? I mean their walk or journey seems so much more exciting than yours? You admire them. You see their accomplishments. You recognize their giftings.

We've all watched little girls parade around in Mom's high heels! They have to grow into them. And even then, they may not be the right size.

PONDERING MY JOURNEY

I did once years ago. Tried to walk in some big shoes. I didn't get more than a few paces.

I greatly esteemed the Episcopal priest, Forrest Mobley. He was highly anointed, well-loved, humble, and had seen miracles happen—even people healed when he prayed for them. While I admired him, I certainly was not jealous of his walk. He had been instrumental in introducing me to the Holy Spirit's empowerment in 1972 when I'd visited my mom in the Florida fishing village of Destin.

As a pastor he was often down at the docks on weekdays praying for fishermen—dressed in a casual shirt and slacks, always wearing his big cross. But on Sundays at St. Andrews Church he donned white vestments, led his kneeling congregation in prayer, then preached powerful sermons. Many people were baptized with the Holy Spirit there during the early days of the renewal movement when Forrest prayed for them, including me. Many believers came, some travelling from other states to worship and receive prayer.

One of the church's first healings happened when a special service was held to pray for Bill Lance, a 31-year-old Air Force captain with acute leukemia which doctors believed was terminal. Forrest anointed Bill with oil, as he and other men gathered around, all joining their prayers of faith. And God did heal Bill in a miraculous way. The good news is that Bill Lance is still alive.

Forrest and his wife Nancy and I became friends though I only saw them when I spent summers at my mom's place. One afternoon when I was visiting them in their home, the phone in the other room rang. Forrest kicked off his shoes and hurried to answer it. As Nancy and I kept talking, I pushed my feet into his big brown loafers and began to walk around the room. She and I both chuckled loudly. Those shoes were way too big for me—they swallowed my smaller feet. Definitely not mine to wear.

"It felt weird, strange, uncomfortable," I told her. "I couldn't walk in these, for sure."

"No, but you have your own shoes to wear—your own unique path to walk. We all have a road to travel, and God equips us with what we need to walk it," Nancy replied.

When Forrest returned, he laughed with us trying to picture me walking in his shoes.

After he left Destin, Forrest served churches in other places and even became dean of a cathedral. But in our retirement years we ended up back in the same Destin, Florida area. By then he was an Anglican priest. During the last six years of his life, he joined my writing critique class. I was still helping him write a book about his Destin church experiences when he slipped into heaven while clutching his "comfort" cross. He died during the pandemic but not of Covid.

But oh, the glorious memories I have, spanning many years of friendship. When I underwent surgery for breast cancer, he was in the hospital waiting room praying. Whenever I'd start writing a new book, he prayed for me. Twice he let me accompany him when he was making visits to housebound parishioners.

He even drove over 400 miles to our home in Titusville to help dedicate our home to the Lord—praying in every room and anointing the doors with oil. This was before we joined Peter Lord's congregation.

Forrest and I had different paths. Wore different shoes. But it was mighty wonderful whenever our paths crossed.

Recalling the day I tried on Forrest's shoes, I am reminded of this Scripture: "And how shall they preach unless they are sent? As it is written 'How beautiful are the feet of those who preach the gospel of peace, who bring glad tidings of good things.'" (Romans 10:15 NKJV)

I can't walk in another person's shoes. And no one can walk in mine. That goes for each of us. Everyone is unique. Paul reminds us: "For we are His workmanship, created in Christ Jesus for good works, which God prepared beforehand that we should walk in them." (Ephesians 2:10 NKJV)

In my "Reflections" (Part Seven), you will read a more detailed account about how important Forrest Mobley was in my spiritual growth. My book *The Beginner's Guide to Receiving the Holy Spirit* has a longer version of what he taught.

Prayer: Thank You, Lord, for showing us what our giftings are and enabling us to fulfill Your purpose for us individually. Thank You for allowing Jesus to live on earth and give us an example of how to walk in ways pleasing to You. In His name we pray. Amen.

Scriptures: "Wear shoes that are able to speed you on as you preach the Good News of peace with God." (Ephesians 6:15 TLB)

"Even before we were born, God planned in advance our destiny and the good works we would do to fulfill it!" (Ephesians 2:10b TPT)

"Stand therefore...having shod your feet with the preparation of the gospel of peace... praying always with all prayer and supplication in the Spirit, being watchful to this end with all perseverance and supplication for all the saints." (Ephesians 6:15,18 NKJV)

Appreciate Dutch Sheets

Dutch Sheets is one pastor whose friendship and mentorship I treasure. An internationally known author and speaker, influencer of many, his daily broadcast and written posts *Give Him 15* reach millions in many nations. He was my beloved pastor ten years (1993-2003) in Colorado Springs where I was ordained into the ministry in 1994.

We were first introduced to him when our children, students at Christ for the Nations Institute in Dallas, sent us his cassette teaching tapes on prayer. He was one of their instructors. We listened to those lessons over and over.

Finally, when we got all our kids through college and then Bible School, LeRoy felt we should go as students to CFNI ourselves. So, we sold our house, loaded up a U-Haul trailer with just enough furniture to fill a small apartment on campus and headed from Florida to Dallas one extremely cold January. We were probably the oldest students there. We spent almost three years at CFNI where he was a full-time student and I audited as many classes as I could. Ruthanne Garlock and I finished writing one book and almost finished a second as she lived in the next apartment building on CFNI campus.

While there my husband and I attended the same church in Dallas where Dutch and Ceci were active. Then Dutch moved to Colorado Springs with a mandate from God to write a book on prayer. But he was also a pastor. After LeRoy's graduation Dutch invited us to come be part of their church fellowship. And we gladly packed another U-Haul trailer with furniture and headed west.

I could never thank Dutch enough for his support of my ministry—always willing to pray for my latest book during church services. Fellowships at his home with his gracious wife Ceci were inspiring as we met monthly with 20 others from the church who were in ministry to encourage and pray for one another.

During this time, I served on the board of directors for Women's Aglow Fellowship (now Aglow International) requiring travels to Seattle headquarters from time to time. Dutch became an advisor for Aglow and a popular speaker at Aglow conventions.

It was my privilege to encourage Dutch to finish that book he had gone to Colorado to write. I'd give him notebooks all the time—one for his car, one for his nightstand, one for his pocket, one for his office, one to take to the mountain cabin hideaway. I prayed diligently for his book to come forth and encouraged him to finish.

Ruthanne Garlock, co-writer of 20 books with Quin, as they met Dutch Sheets at his Alabama conference.

What a privilege to finally hold that book in my hand. *Intercessory Prayer* is now a classic, being read by thousands! And he has gone on to write more than 20 other books since then. Proud of him? Yes. But I am so grateful for his touch on my life too.

One day not long after *Intercessory Prayer* was published, a woman, seated next to me on an airplane out of Miami, told me she was a missionary in the deep jungles of Argentina. After three years there she was now flying to her sister's in Houston to get a physical. She had received a copy of *Intercessory Prayer* and if I knew anything about that book, she wanted to discuss it. I had a delightful time showing her in my Bible what Dutch had written about. I was happy to learn that his book had found its way even to her remote jungle setting and had caused her to have a spiritual hunger. When I got home, I mailed a box full of other books to her Houston address for her to take back to Argentina.

Dutch was willing to get "out of the box" for our church's worship services. One summer on three different occasions we moved to a downtown park to have Sunday worship—musicians took their instruments, the worship team took their banners, and the congregation brought picnic lunches to share after services with any homeless people who came to hear the service.

We'd have all night prayer meetings. Youth gatherings. Once we joined other congregations for an awesome worship service in the chapel at the Air Force Academy.

He used to say one of the goals of our church was to make it "a house of prayer for the nation" and I felt he was helping us accomplish that.

Most of us from Dutch's congregation got involved in the prayer ministry held at the newly established World Prayer Center—taking turns on the prayer vigils. Dr. C. Peter Wagner was key in helping direct vision for the World Prayer Center which drew intercessors, missionaries, and spiritual leaders from all parts of the world to attend classes, worship, and most of all to pray. I had the privilege to teach at Wagner Institute at the World Prayer Center. Worship services there on Wednesdays at noon when musician Terry MacAlmon led worship were absolutely glorious.

I remember Dutch saying, "God does unexpected things in unexpected ways, in unexpected times, through unexpected people."

After ten years in Colorado, my husband and I moved back to Northwest Florida. But my friendship with Dutch and Ceci continued. I even had the honor of writing a few of his devotional posts for *Give Him 15*. And whenever I did, I heard from folks I knew in England, Japan, and all over the U.S. Today, his broadcasts reach millions.

Quin and Dutch Sheets pray together. He was her pastor in Colorado Springs 10 years while she was an intercessor for him when he wrote his classic book **Intercessory Prayer**, *and many that followed.*

Dutch opened doors of opportunity for me to speak across this nation and I am most grateful for the blessing he and Ceci have been to me. Thanks to them I had the most spectacular surprise 90th birthday party!

Prayer: Lord, thank You for faithful pastors and friends who stand by you in prayer and are there to encourage you when circumstances in your life get tough. Bless them abundantly! In Jesus' name I ask. Amen.

Scripture: "And He Himself gave some to be apostles, some prophets, some evangelists, and some pastors and teachers, for the equipping of the saints for the work of ministry, for the edifying of the body of Christ, till we all come to the unity of the faith and of the knowledge of the Son of God." (Ephesians 4:11-14 NKJV)

Catching What Was Taught

After a 20-year absence, I was honored to be invited back to my former church pastored by Peter Lord as their women's retreat speaker. To the church where women had mentored me when I was a mom with three teenagers. I was asked to speak on the topic of one of my books, *A House of Many Blessings*.

I realized I had come full circle—now I was a grandmother coming to encourage a younger generation of women who love the Lord.

At the last session I spoke to the 300 in attendance on hospitality and mentoring. As I ended my final speech, I paid tribute to some of the women from my past now seated at our roundtable. As I introduced them and had them stand, I proudly acknowledged how each had influenced me those years gone by.

Mary Jo had brought her team to decorate my home and then I had taken "before" and "after" photos of the other homes she decorated to give slide presentations to other women's groups throughout the state—encouraging them to multiply this ministry of helps. She was the first one to encourage me to speak publicly in front of others at a Bible study.

Margaret had been the more mature woman in our church home group that met weekly at my house and had not only encouraged me in spiritual things but had taught one of my daughters how to be a better seamstress and another to bake bread. Lib had prayed faithfully with me on the phone for five minutes every weekday morning for many years. Liz, owner of a flower shop, had tried to teach me to make arrangements, but was mostly my "let's have fun" pal who always made me laugh. Barbara, Louise, and Anne stood, and I mentioned others who were unable to be there as I listed their giftings which had also figured heavily in my growth—casting their shadows on my life as influencers. I thanked them all and sat down to eat lunch.

We had just started on our dessert when a young woman came to our table and asked if she could address us "older" women. Those sitting with her in the back corner were from a church in another city, she said. Yet they had made an important decision just now. We urged her to tell us.

She explained: "When we heard how you have been friends all these years—even when one moved away—and how you have continued to pray for one another, we were touched. We made a commitment today to do the same. We want to keep lifelong friendships like you have had, and we want to pray for each other too. Thank you for a great show-and-tell lesson."

Most of us "oldies" choked back tears. "They caught what we taught," Mary Jo said as she flashed me a big grin.[14]

Some years later, when Mary Jo had turned 90, I traveled 450 miles to visit her. I had truly come full circle now, sitting once again at her feet listening to wisdom as she talked. And I learned she was still mentoring young women who came to her house.

The next year when the call came that she had left this earth, I smiled remembering all the ways she had touched my life. For more than 30 years she had called me on my birthday and had mailed me a card with a two-dollar bill tucked inside. I have an envelope full of those dollars. What's more, she did the same for those other women she had mentored. What an influencer. What a shadow she cast over me.

One author described what Mary Jo was to me: "So if you want to unlock your hidden potential, spend your time with people who will stretch you. Find somebody who thinks faster, runs faster, and aims higher. Those are the people who will lift you up."[15]

She truly did that for me.

---

[14] Quin Sherrer, *Good Night, Lord*. (Ventura, CA: Regal Books, 2002), 241.
[15] John Maxwell, *Be All You Can Be*. (Colorado Springs, CO: Victor, a division of Cook Publishing, 2002, originally published 1987), 29.

Prayer: Thank You, Lord for those who inspire us and encourage us in our daily walks. Bless them. May those who they taught continue to share those nuggets with others. Amen.

Scripture: "For as we have many members in one body, but all the members do not have the same function, so we, being many, are one body in Christ, and individually members of one another." (Romans 12:4-5 KJV)

People in Ministry Whom I Heard Speak or Knew Personally

Derek and Lydia Prince, David du Plessis, Rita and Dennis Bennett, Shirley Dobson, Dick and Dee Eastman, Corrie ten Boom, John and Elizabeth Sherrill, Katherine Kuhlman, Oral Roberts, Chuck and Pam Pierce, Paul Billheimer, Kenneth Copeland, John Dawson, Joy Dawson, John and Diana Hagee, Jamie and Jackie Buckingham, Fuchsia Pickett, Catherine Marshall, Len LeSourd, Tommy Tenney, Che Ahn, Jack Hayford, Freda Lindsay, Peter and Johnnie Lord, Dutch and Ceci Sheets, Peter and Doris Wagner, Cindy and Mike Jacobs, Lou Engle, John Wimber, John and Carol Arnott, Benny Hinn, Joyce Myers, Kay Arthur, Bill Bright, Beth Alves, Dee Jepsen, James and Michal Ann Goll, John and Ruthanne Garlock, Reinhard Bonnke, Martha Lucia, Jane Hamon, Bishop Bill Hamon, Barbara Yoder, Jane Hansen Hoyt, Max Lucado, Pat Robertson, Phil Saint, Cheryl Sacks, Pauline Parham (Charles Parham's daughter-in-law), Mrs. Norman Vincent Peale, Arthur Gordon, Marilyn Hickey, Wayne Myers, Mary Lance Sisk, Forrest and Nancy Mobley, Rachel Burchfield, Mickie Winborn, JoAnne Bailey, Barbara James, Mary Jo Pierce, Barbara Wentroble, Marion Bond West, Germaine Copeland, Lisa Bevere, JoNell Gerland, Sherry Anderson, Brenda Kilpatrick, Mary Glazier, Mary Forsythe, Beth Clark, Faye Mays, Ken Malone, Terry MacAlmon, Eddie and Alice Smith, David Wilkerson, and many others.

(Hearing speakers does not mean I agreed with everything each taught.)

Part Six: Mentoring Others

Keeper Friends Are Treasures

Who are the people outside your family who stand out as some of the greatest influencers in your life? Probably your closest friends? I know it is true for me.

Friends. Genuine "Keeper Friends" are there for you when you need encouragement, sympathy, comfort, support. You often shadow one another. At times you both may sacrifice for the benefit and good of the other.

Supportive friendships hold each other accountable. Sometimes schedules will need rearranging. Friendships cost time, respect, agape love, and plenty of prayer, but genuine friends are worth all the effort.

One of my longer friendships began after church one Sunday when Lib, a woman I had never met, invited my family to her house for Sunday dinner. There was a catch. "I don't have enough food for all of us, but we could share," she told me. "You look like someone I'd really like to get to know. Besides our children would enjoy some new friends too."

I never imagined what I was getting into that Sunday we lugged our dinner to Lib's house and spread it outdoors on a picnic table. The next week her family came to our home, bringing their dinner. We did this every Sunday after church for over a year. We were shy young moms living in tiny box houses on shoestring budgets

PONDERING MY JOURNEY

while our husbands worked crazy shifts at Florida's newly established Space Center and were often gone days at a time. Between us we had seven children near the same ages. Lib and I were born the same week and the same year. Sisters in the Lord.

As our friendship blossomed and our relationship with the Lord grew stronger, we decided we needed to pray for our children on a regular basis. So, at exactly 8:00 a.m., we prayed together on the phone, for just five minutes, every weekday morning for many incredible years. Our families grew close too, often camping together on summer weekends. When my husband took early retirement in 1980 and we moved, Lib and I still kept in touch by phone. Then many years later on a Mother's Day weekend her husband and four sons buried her between a giant oak and a blooming gardenia tree. "She, who loved flowers and plants, would have approved," one son wrote me.

When LeRoy retired from NASA, we moved close to Destin to be near Mother. Since we still had two kids in college, he worked with a construction company as a building supervisor. I yearned for a prayer partner like I had with Lib. One day in our new church I finally asked Fran Ewing whom I'd met there if she would pray with me on a regular basis. I really desired to pray with this woman who had been led to the Lord by the Dutch evangelist/holocaust survivor Corrie ten Boom some years earlier. In fact, over a long period Corrie spent some time between her speaking engagements at the homes of Fran and Mike writing books and enjoying their various activities, even though they lived in three different states during that time span. She called their home her "hiding place" and asked that her bedroom be left exactly like it was, so it felt like home whenever she and her nurse assistant Ellen came to spend time there.

Fran finally said "yes" to becoming a prayer partner but added that she'd like to invite four other women friends from the church to join us at her house from 5:30 to 6:30 on Monday mornings. Which is what we did—for the next three years. We prayed primarily for our individual families. Afterwards when the other women left, Fran and I spent another hour together, talking, praying, and often eating breakfast together.

Once in the middle of the night Fran phoned members of our praying group from an Atlanta hospital where an oncology doctor had told them that their son was not expected to live through the night. We women got out of bed and walked the floor—crying out to God on behalf of Mark. It was touch and go for some days. He not only survived, but he also became the father of two sons, another miracle from God. Today he is still alive—thanks to the healing power of our Lord.

When my mother died, Fran sang the solos at her funeral. I can almost still hear her clear soprano voice singing about Jesus, "How Great Thy Art." Her husband, Mike, had been a doctor in the military when polio left much of his body paralyzed. He became my husband's best friend and Fran became mine for 35 years. Sitting with her on her front porch rockers in 1985, I wrote on my first book, *How to Pray for Your Children*, while she prayed and edited my rough manuscript. Even when we lived elsewhere, I would return to visit her.

My husband and I finally returned to the Destin area in 2004. For the last eleven years of her life, we enjoyed each other's company. However, for six of those latter years Fran was on dialysis. If your kidneys cannot keep your blood filtered and purified, dialysis performs the function of your kidneys using a machine—often for four hours at a time. I sometimes drove her for her treatments which she underwent several times a week.

On the day after Thanksgiving in 2015 she was in the hospital and undergoing dialysis. She dialed me on her cell phone. "I am short of breath—call intercessors," she whispered. Twenty minutes later she met her Savior Jesus face to face. And I lost one of the best friends I ever had.

PONDERING MY JOURNEY

Quin waiting with praying friends Fran and Tommie to do a radio interview in Pensacola.

Then there was Tommie in Destin. For years she was only a phone call away to pray with me. We took exciting ministry trips together, two overseas. When my husband passed away, she was with me and two years later I sat many hours at her bedside before she joined him in heaven.

Over the years I have "collected" some wonderful female friends who have offered me nurturing emotional support, advice, counsel, encouragement, and prayer coverage. In turn, I have done the same for them.

One of my most memorable was Dee Eastman, whose husband, Dick, was President of Every Home for Christ in Colorado Springs where we lived from 1993-2003. During those ten years when we were both in town, we met on Tuesday mornings at the ministry's headquarters to pray for our nation and other countries. Often, we moved to what I called the "war room"—a special room of maps and notes to help one pray for missionaries and countries the ministry sponsored. After our hour of prayer, we usually went to a Mexican restaurant for lunch and laughs. At various Christian conferences we'd room together. On my 90th birthday she called me in Florida to remind me of those wonderful days.

Outside a Christian women's leadership meeting in windy Dallas—Suzanne, JoNell, Quin, and Mary Jo enjoy a laugh. Each travelled with Quin to her various speaking events, often driving her there.

In more recent years Dr. Faye Mays, a retired educator, has driven me up and down the streets of our town on prayer journeys. We pray over schools, businesses, churches, police and fire stations, city hall, banks, and other sites. We particularly pray at places where our family members work. I might give her an unexpected early morning call, "Faye, we got to hit the road in prayer today." Before long she'll be at my house ready for a two or three-hour prayer drive. We have even prayed together in Tallahassee for our state and in Washington D.C. for our nation while attending the same prayer gatherings.

PONDERING MY JOURNEY

Dr. Faye Mays, Quin's prayer partner, arrives to take her on another prayer drive through their town.

Quin prays over Mary Forsythe's new Bible Study book that will even be read by women in prisons.

While my many friends and I have seen each other through trials and heartaches, we have also had a lot of laughs. Mary Jo, JoNell, Kerry, Beth, Mary, Ceci, Kate, Sherry, Jane, Faye, Elizabeth, Brenda, Sally, Ruthanne, Jeanette, Cindy, Dee, Dorothea, Mary Beth, Suzanne, Lilia, Denise, Lori, Anne, Bee, and others.

God knew how I needed the unique giftedness of all my special friends. Among them are writers, widows, homemakers, grandmothers, and career gals. To keep our friendships vital, we keep in touch via phone, text, or email. These Keepers live in nine different states. There is no distance in prayer or even in friendships. Amid our family's challenges, steadfast friends have covered us with prayer and encouragement. Once several called us in the middle of a hurricane before our phones went dead.

Not all Keeper friendships are at the same level of reciprocation. You may find some friends have less time than others to keep in touch. Some are busy moms. Some have full-time jobs. Others travel with work or ministries. Some are active community volunteers. Some are caregivers to ailing spouses or parents. Others babysit grandchildren. And the list goes on.

I hope you have some "Keeper Friends" too. If you don't, ask God to help you find them. You will be blessed! Friends are great treasures, never to be taken for granted.

Prayer: Lord, thank You for the gift of friends, especially those I count on who love and support me in trying times as well as smooth-sailing ones. Help me remember to thank them for their faithfulness. Help me to be a very faithful friend to them too. I pray in the name of Jesus, Amen.

Scripture: "Be kindly affectionate to one another with brotherly love, in honor giving preference to one another." (Romans 12:10 NKJV)

PONDERING MY JOURNEY

JoAnne's Lessons

As I write this my dear friend JoAnne is physically on earth, but she is heavenly minded—anxious to go see her Savior. Ever since I have known her JoAnne has longed for heaven but has spent much of her waking hours in the King's Army on earth—praying, preaching, cooking for others. When she turned 90 in February, she was very ill—so bedridden she couldn't turn herself over in bed. We thought surely she'd be graduated by then.

Some of my last conversations with her as her husband held the phone to her ear went like this: JoAnne in a whispered voice, "Join me in heaven. I am so excited to be going there finally."

I answered, "I ain't ready to go yet. My mother and husband can greet you—I have much more work to do here. I love you and I promise your legacy will live on in me."

She had been my mother's prayer partner in Florida in the late 1970s when her Air Force doctor husband was stationed in Florida. Then in 1980, they got transferred to Wiesbaden, Germany. I visited them three years later. When she returned to the States, our friendship continued long-distance. We'd meet at Christian conferences. Then she began to drive me to my speaking engagements all over the U.S. We took a month-long trip to Europe where I spoke in four countries, and she served as my prayer intercessor and travelling companion.

She had a happy occasion while still living in Germany. On January 20, 1981, after Ronald Reagan's inauguration as the 40th president of the United States, the 52 U.S. captives held at the U.S. embassy in Tehran, Iran, were released, ending the 444-day Iran hostage crisis. They were first taken to Germany for medical exams and treatment before coming home. JoAnne's husband, George, was one of the doctors who treated them. She was thrilled to dance with a few of those military men at an event in their honor. She had prayed continuously for their release from captivity so in essence she was dancing with an answer to her prayers.

One time after JoAnne moved back to the States, she and I met in New York to fly to Germany for some speaking engagements. The man sitting next to me on the plane told me his dad was occupying the aisle seat across from him. He and his mother were trying to get him back to their home in the Middle East because he had undergone lung surgery in Houston. But into the night the ailing dad grew worse. An hour and a half before we landed in Frankfurt where they needed to change planes, he quietly died. Some passengers sitting nearby went into what I called the "crazy panic mode" by chattering loudly, while others demanded to be moved. One airline attendant was crying, even while trying to calm or reseat passengers.

JoAnne and I prayed quietly for peace and calm to come out of the confusion. She began to sing in her prayer language, then to hum some well-known hymns. Quickly the atmosphere changed. Peace seemed to permeate our portion of the cabin. People stopped demanding attention from airline attendants. I tried to comfort the son as his eyes focused on his dad's body which was now covered in a sheet. His mom continued to sit next to her deceased husband, quietly grieving. JoAnne and I continued praying silently for them.

I never had a friend who prayed as much as JoAnne did for the ministry leaders on her "prayer list"—but she did for years. Sometimes for six hours straight. And she was usually her pastor's chief intercessor, no matter where they lived. She was known as "the prayer warrior."

Another time while attending a Christian conference in Milwaukee, she wanted us to have an afternoon cup of tea. As we sat at a counter in an old-fashioned drug store, she began to tell me of a recent miracle healing story she had heard on a Christian television program. I asked pertinent questions to get the full picture. A man sitting two seats down from us held a newspaper

PONDERING MY JOURNEY

in front of his face. Obviously, he was not reading it, but was listening to JoAnne tell how Jesus is still doing miracles today.

JoAnne who travelled twice with Quin through Europe as she spoke and drove her to many places in the States as her very effective prayer intercessor.

Suddenly the man threw the newspaper across the counter and loudly shouted, "All right, already, I will get baptized. Sunday, I will." And he ran out of the drug store. JoAnne and I looked at each other in amazement. We offered a short prayer for the man who was obviously on his way back to the Lord.

Lessons I Learned from JoAnne:

- Let humor get you through the roughest of times—the joy of the Lord is your strength.
- Make do with what you have and be thankful. Stay prepared for hard times ahead.
- Don't give in to distractions. Whenever she drove me on my speaking tours we left even before daybreak. We

didn't stop along the way wandering through antique stores, or coffee shops, or other inviting places. Keep your eye on the destination and don't get distracted was her motto. But on our way home from those meetings, we had a grand time exploring fun places.
- Never miss an opportunity to tell an individual how much Jesus wants to be his/her Savior because He loves us all. Win as many people to Jesus as you can!
- Pray in your prayer language more often.

Prayer: Thank You Lord for faithful friends who stand with us through trials and triumphs. Thank You for how they impart hope and faith to us by the way they live their lives. Thank You most of all for Jesus, who loves us unconditionally. Amen.

Scripture: "The righteous should choose his friends carefully, For the way of the wicked leads them astray." (Proverbs 12:26 NKJV)

Mentoring Lessons Last Long

A couple of years ago just a few days before Christmas I pulled up to a service station on a late Saturday afternoon to put gas in my car. Suddenly, a man appeared at my window—behind him stood a woman and three young children, all wearing T-shirts with the name of a local church on them.

"Sorry, I didn't mean to startle you, but we want to fill up your gas tank as a Christmas gift to you," he said.

"Why?" I asked him.

"A couple named Skip and Linda Evans taught me to do this at Christmastime some years ago," he explained. What an unexpected surprise! Just a few months earlier I attended my friend Skip's memorial service.

I learned that those youth who attended the Evans' Bible study group years ago were given cash at Christmastime to do acts of kindness and bless others. This young man had chosen to gas up cars of older people —and the lesson he had learned from the Evanses never left him.

And what an unexpected blessing I received. What were the chances that someone who knew Linda and Skip would be the ones to receive such a gift? I called Linda to tell her what had just happened, thanking her for giving me gas this Christmas. She was pleasantly surprised and blessed on this first year without her beloved husband to learn that this young man was still practicing what she and Skip had taught him long ago. Now he was teaching these youngsters. Mentoring? Of course.

Prayer: Jesus, please help me be more aware of the people I influence by what I say and how I act. Forgive me for the many times I have not done this in a Christ-honoring way. I am truly sorry, and I choose to better represent my faith in You as my Lord. Amen.

Scripture: "And remember the words of the Lord Jesus, that He said, 'It is more blessed to give than to receive.'" (Acts 20:35b NKJV)

An Extra Child to Love

Sometimes God sends people into our lives by divine appointment, and from then on, they seem like family—extended family, at least.

One Sunday our pastor Peter Lord announced, "Jesus needs some innkeepers." He explained that some young people were coming as interns to work with our youth for a year and they needed housing. We volunteered to be house parents to one of them.

When Mike called to accept our invitation to join our family, I phoned Johnnie, our pastor's wife, for some advice, since she had been a foster mom to several boys his age. Her guidelines were helpful to me.

"Make him part of the family immediately by giving him responsibilities—like making his bed and washing his own clothes. Plan things together as a family and be sure he knows he's included, whether he can make it or not. Make time for him just as you would your own children. Let him know you love him as he is but correct him in love when necessary. Let him be free to bring his friends to your home, for it is now his home."

"He will be a blessing to you, and God will honor your obedience to love and serve Him through Mike," she added.

He was 23 when he bounced into our lives to bring us much joy and fun. He looked like a young Abe Lincoln with his dark beard and six-foot-three, slightly bent frame.

Mike would roughhouse with our teenage son (with whom he shared a room), play the guitar for our morning family devotions, talk me into hosting 60 kids from the church's youth group at our house for a party, and leave his smelly tennis shoes perched on our dining room table occasionally.

He was flexible, funny, and uncomplaining. He lived with us for more than a year. I prayed a lot for him, especially that God would give him a wife. Robin, a gifted schoolteacher who volunteered with the youth group, was the answer to that prayer. And when they had children, Robin homeschooled. Mike eventually went to seminary and became a compassionate pastor.

I'll never forget the letter he wrote us ten years after he'd lived with us as our adopted son. He thanked each member of our family for what he or she had meant in his life. I cried bucketfuls as I read it.

Our enjoyable experience as surrogate parents to Mike led us later to open our small Dallas apartment in 1990 to special young people while we—as the oldest Bible students on Christ for the Nations campus—served them food, love, and counsel. And sometimes paid their late tuition fees. Our three kids had already graduated from there so some of the second-year students had been their friends.

PONDERING MY JOURNEY

One who became like our beloved adopted daughter, Sharona, was born in Israel, and at the age of 20 had already explored 20 countries. After Bible school, she stayed on in Dallas to complete a degree at another college. She still came over almost every weekend to either eat or spend the night with us, bringing laughter, love, and song into our lives.

In our campus kitchen I kept a prayer board filled with pictures of all our adopted kids there, some of whom had left after their graduation to serve the Lord in missions overseas. Sharona made us a sign in Hebrew to hang above that picture board: MISHPACHA—Our Family. Our extended family.[16]

Then there was David who walked the track with me five days a week and came to our apartment often to help cook. Recently he and his wife, Leah, drove from Mississippi to visit me in Florida. Sharona just sent an email greeting from Italy where she lives while her husband directs an art study abroad for Christian college students.

Sunday chapel services at Christ for the Nations were in the afternoons at 2:00 p.m.—required attendance. Students were encouraged to attend a church in Dallas on Sunday mornings. It was my custom to have four or five students over for lunch before chapel services on campus. But those who sat at our table had to tell me a "take-away" from the sermon they heard at whatever church they attended that morning. Was I mentoring? Yes, perhaps, but it got those students really listening to the pastor's sermon.

Prayer: Lord, thank You for extended family. For some people it means aunts, uncles, cousins, grandparents. For us it is that but also the many young people You brought into our lives and homes. Thank You for the delight of knowing them and for their unique contribution to our family. I pray that each will continue to experience Your direction, provision, protection, peace, and

---

[16] Quin Sherrer, *Good Night, Lord*. (Ventura, CA: Regal Books, 2002), 84-86.

presence. I pray this too for all our kinfolk—our natural family members of all ages. I ask in the name of Jesus. Amen.

Scriptures: "Contribute to the needs of the saints." (Romans 12:13)

"Be hospitable to one another without complaint." (1 Peter 4:9)

Let Us Mentor and Influence Others

Wouldn't our sphere of influence be enriched if each of us would mentor another person? Just to encourage someone in practical and spiritual ways, passing down our experience, knowledge, and wisdom on a one-on-one basis?

My definition of mentoring is simple: to encourage and equip for excellence—passing down knowledge and training to one who is less experienced, helping that person reach her God-given potential.

I like this definition, "A mentor is someone further down the road from you who is willing to hold the light to help you get there."[17]

Don't overlook the opportunity to mentor others online when person-to-person meetings are impossible. Pray about such a possibility.

My first advice is to be yourself, using your own special gifts. Don't be afraid to mentor out of your own trials and failures as well as your triumphs. Thank God every day for the creative gifts He has put within you and be a good steward of them.

You will set your own mentoring guidelines, but some I have used include:

Discuss goals with your mentee.

What does she/he want to learn from you?

---

[17] Win Couchman, quoted in Dee Brestin, *The Friendship of Women*. (Wheaton, IL: Victor Books, 1989), 162.

PONDERING MY JOURNEY

Quin praying with a mentee (Cara, on right) and her prayer partner (Anna) at a meeting in Dallas.

Decide when and how often you will be in contact (once a week, once a month).

Will you study a certain book?

Does the mentee need to purchase special tools to learn/improve a skill you will be teaching?

Pray for those you mentor as they learn to apply new things.

Teach in such a way that each person can later mentor others.

Make it a fun learning experience too.

Peter advised: "As each one has received a gift, minister it to one another, as good stewards of the manifold grace of God." (1 Peter 4:10 NKJV)

Paul wrote, "As for the things you have learned and received and heard and seen in me, practice these things, and the God of peace will be with you." (Philippians 4:9 NASB)

Jamie Buckingham, my writing mentor, quoted a Scripture to me: "To whom much is given, much will be required" (Luke 12:48 NKJV). It was my mandate to teach what he and others had taught me. As well as sharing from my own experiences.

Over the years I have been blessed by being mentored and by mentoring others. Computers and smart phones have become helpful devices for me to use in mentoring those who don't live nearby. Up for the challenge? Let's go do it!

I wrote this prayer in our latest book, *Warfare Prayers for Women*, for older women to pray who want to mentor younger ones.

Prayer: Lord, we seniors have a wealth of wisdom, knowledge, and experience we could share with younger women. Our talent and skills for certain tasks should not be wasted just because we are older. Open the door to opportunities for me to help others succeed in their callings. If there are younger women You want me to mentor, please bring them my way and help us connect our generations. I want to be an encourager, a prayer partner, a teacher to impart something positive into a few women coming behind me. I refuse the enemy's interference in God's chosen plan for our meeting and mutually learning from one another. Thank You, Lord, for the ways You will cause this to happen. May I be vigilant to share more about Your love and Your desire to equip us to do Your will. Amen.[18]

Scripture: "Therefore encourage one another and build each other up, just as in fact you are doing." (1 Thessalonians 4:11)

---

[18] Quin Sherrer and Ruthanne Garlock, *Warfare Prayers for Women*. (Bloomington, MN: Chosen Books, 2020), 194.

Part Seven: Spiritual Reflections

Holy Spirit's Visitation

I had no idea how much my life was going to change—and for the better—the summer of 1972 when it was time to once again take my three children and go visit Mom in Destin, Florida.

On a Thursday night she insisted that I go with her to the new church she'd started attending—St. Andrews By-the-Sea Episcopal. The Thursday evening worship service was so foreign to me. Men and women raised their hands in praise to God. They even sang Scripture choruses, straight from the Bible.

The pews were full, and people stood in the aisles worshipping God. As a journalist I tried to figure out what was going on. While it was so different from anything I had experienced before, I recognized I was sitting in a holy atmosphere. These people knew Jesus in a depth I did not. I watched in amazement as a grown man with hands upraised, began softly praising the Lord with tears rolling down his cheeks. "Jesus, I love You. Thank You for dying for me, for my sins."

Leaving the service, I introduced myself to the pastor, Rev. Forrest Mobley. Swallowing my pride, I asked him, "What makes these people so different from me and other Christians I know? I've taught Sunday School most of my adult life, and Jesus is my Savior, but I don't worship like these folks. How can I do it?"

"Most of these who come to worship on Thursday night have received the baptism in the Holy Spirit—the gift Jesus told His followers He would send before He went to heaven," he told me.

"You mean I can receive this gift too?" I asked.

"Of course, you can," he responded. "After our Thursday night worship meetings, those who are interested in more instruction can come to my office. After I teach, then I pray for them to be filled with power—or as Jesus called it 'baptized with the Holy Spirit.'"

"Well, if you are serious, reread the first four chapters of Acts, then come ask me more questions next Thursday. But read with an open mind, asking God to reveal truth to you," he added.

The next night I attended a home prayer meeting where a group from St. Andrews had gathered. As about a dozen of us sat praying, the shrill ring of the telephone distracted my attention. Betty Moore, our hostess, slipped out of the room to answer as the rest in the room kept praying. Everyone except me. Being unaccustomed to praying aloud, I just sat there listening.

Some were praying softly in languages I'd never heard before. Others were thanking God for healing a man named Bill. These people talked to God as if they knew Him intimately. I envied that, yet it bewildered me. Betty returned and softly announced, "That was a message about Bill Lance. The doctors at the military hospital in Mississippi say he may die tonight of acute leukemia. Let's pray in agreement right now for his life to be spared."

Then Betty prayed aloud, "Lord, we believe You are restoring him. Regardless of what the doctors say. So, we stand in agreement and thank You in advance for his healing."

A man in the room spoke aloud, "Bill Lance is God's property, and we are standing in the gap for his complete healing. Spirits of infirmity leave him, in Jesus' name." Now, that was a new strategy to me.

Betty leaned toward me and quietly explained that Bill Lance was a new Christian, a 31-year-old Air Force captain stationed at a nearby Florida base. "The doctors say he is in critical condition, so prayer groups all over town are being called. Yet, we've had assurance that God is going to heal Bill. He's got the assurance too, so we'll keep on praying. A few weeks ago, there was a special healing service at our church for him as our pastor, Forrest Mobley, and elders laid hands on him and prayed for his healing—just like in the New Testament."

Here I was, a Christian at a home prayer meeting, not sure about healing in such a crisis situation. "Lord, hear their prayers," I prayed silently. "Listen to Betty and to all their prayers. I don't know whether You still heal or not. So, count my doubt out. But Lord show me truth."

I was puzzled. Even though I had been healed of malaria as a teenager, I had not seen miraculous healings since so I had decided healing must have gone out with the apostles like my denomination taught. And what about Paul's teaching in the New Testament about speaking in tongues? Yet tonight I sensed something dynamic in the way these people believed and prayed.

Before the meeting ended, I was sure I wanted to know Jesus as personally as they did. Jesus was my Savior—my passport to heaven, so to speak—but I had to admit that I had not allowed Him to be Lord of my life. Furthermore, I wanted to pray and praise God in my own prayer language.

The following Thursday night, I was back at St. Andrews and after the worship service, I joined a handful of others in Pastor Mobley's study for instruction.

"Although His eleven closest disciples had been with Jesus almost constantly for some three years, He still told them and the other followers to stay in the city until you have been clothed with power from on high," Forrest Mobley said, quoting Luke 24:19.

"Why? Because they were going to need the power of the Holy Spirit once Jesus ascended back to heaven," he said.

"Tonight, we are going to pray together, confess our sins, and ask the Holy Spirit to be in charge of our lives. Then you will receive a new prayer language. Praying in tongues bypasses our mind, enabling our spirits to speak directly to God through the Holy Spirit," he continued.

What followed the Bible lesson on the first two chapters of Acts that night in Pastor Mobley's office totally changed my life. He asked each of us to put into our own words a prayer patterned after this one:

"Jesus, I acknowledge You as my Lord and Savior. I ask You to forgive my sins: the wrong things I've done, and the things I've failed to do—the things I remember and those I don't. I choose to forgive all who have hurt or wounded me. I free them from any bondage I've held them in through my unforgiveness. If I have ever made fun of anyone who spoke in tongues, please forgive me, Lord. I receive Your forgiveness for my sins. I renounce any involvement with the occult—whether I participated in it knowingly or unknowingly—including anything related to the kingdom of darkness. I renounce the devil and all his works."

"Lord, I now ask to receive the baptism in the Holy Spirit and to speak in a new tongue. In the name of Jesus Christ, I receive in faith. Amen."

After I audibly forgave my dad for abandoning our family, Pastor Mobley laid hands on me and the others and prayed for us to receive this empowering of the Holy Spirit. I timidly spoke only a few unfamiliar syllables. They sounded so elementary to me. Was this really praying in tongues, or did I make it up? How glad I was for the warning the pastor gave us.

"Don't let the devil tell you that you did not speak in tongues tonight," he cautioned. "God gave you that gift of the Holy Spirit. And just as a baby learns to talk with only a few sounds at first, so your prayer language begins with a few syllables, then it will expand, increase, and often change."

It was a night I would never forget. An overpowering love for God and for people began to engulf me—especially love and forgiveness for my daddy who had deserted Mother when I was barely a teen.

When I left Mom's place to return home a few days later, I was definitely changed. I laughed more; I studied the Bible with a new hunger. I even started praying for close friends to be healed. Amazingly, some were.[19]

Jesus declared that after receiving the Holy Spirit, His followers would have power to be His witnesses (see Acts 1:18). I certainly found this to be true. I couldn't resist "testifying" to what Jesus had done for me and asking people if they wanted me to pray for them for any situations.

The next summer my children and I returned to Destin to visit Mother. The first day I hurried to see Pastor Mobley, excited to tell him all the wonderful things God was doing in my life. He motioned for me to come to his office to meet someone new.

"Meet Bill Lance," he said.

Was this healthy looking 32-year-old man with a full head of hair really the man they were praying for at Betty's last summer? The Air Force captain, a veterinarian, who was dying from acute leukemia? God had healed him?

As Bill shared his story with me, the more Forrest Mobley smiled. Turning to me, he said, "Quin, I think you are to write Bill's testimony. How about letting me pray for you?" As I sat in his office chair, he laid hands on my head, anointed me with oil, and prayed for the Holy Spirit to guide me as I wrote about this, St.

---

[19] Quin Sherrer and Ruthanne Garlock, *The Beginners Guide to Receiving the Holy Spirit*. (Bloomington, MN: Chosen Books, 2011), 29-37.

Andrews' first big healing story. I followed Bill to his home to interview him and Sharon in depth.

After entering my story about Bill's healing in the Guideposts Magazine Writers Workshop contest, God was so gracious to let me be among about 20 in the United States who won that great opportunity—to spend a week in Rye, New York studying under outstanding Christian authors like John and Elizabeth Sherrill, Catherine Marshall, Len LeSourd, Jamie Buckingham, Arthur Gordon, and others.

Rev. Forrest Mobley with Quin and Bill Lance, who was healed of leukemia after Forrest's Episcopal Church prayed for him. Quin's story on Bill won her the 1973 Guideposts Writers Workshop opportunity to go to New York to study under well-known Christian authors.

Back in Titusville, I continued writing for my local newspaper *The Star Advocate* and Christian magazines. And some years later I began to write books for Christian audiences.

I am most grateful for Forrest Mobley's guidance and prayer for me to receive the Holy Spirit's empowerment. And for his suggestion that I write Bill Lance's story. God has continued to use Bill mightily in his career. We talked on the phone the other afternoon—52 years after his touch from God! After his health was restored, Bill demonstrated his love for animals by founding a specialized pharmaceutical company benefiting zoos and free-ranging wildlife worldwide.

His healing story is included in my book *Miracles Happen When You Pray*, a Zondervan publication which later was chosen as one of Guideposts Book Club editions.

Me a doubter? Not anymore. Healing. Signs. Wonders. Prophecy. Interceding in a prayer language. How grateful I am that the Holy Spirit can now come alongside as our Teacher, Comforter, Helper! And especially for assisting us to pray in a prayer language.

Christ, the Hope of Glory

That Christmas week in 1972 when I made my first trip to Israel, airport security was extremely tight. We had been searched meticulously even before we entered the country. But with that behind us, we began our pilgrimage by visiting ancient Biblical sites.

At daybreak on an extremely cold morning, our tour group gathered in a beautifully manicured garden spot outside the main gates of Jerusalem. An open tomb was before us like the one that held the body of Jesus—some believe it is the one. We were here at the Garden Tomb to celebrate His life and resurrection.

After we sang about His rising from the tomb, a pastor delivered a short message. "Remember how you were searched before you came into Israel?" he asked. Did I remember! I was one of few who was given a "body search"—thorough and embarrassing.

PONDERING MY JOURNEY

"You smuggled something into Jerusalem they couldn't take away from you in customs. It's not found in museums or in any of the historical places," he continued.

What was he getting at? I wondered.

"You smuggled Jesus into Jerusalem! They couldn't lock that up. If you know Him, then His Spirit lives within you. The Bible says it is Christ in you, the hope of glory," he said as he read Colossians 1:27 from the Apostle Paul.

"Even the mystery which hath been hid for ages and generations: but now hath it been manifested to his saints, to whom God was pleased to make known what is the riches of the glory of this mystery among the Gentiles, which is Christ in you, the hope of glory." (Colossians 1:26-27 ASV)

I sat contemplating that Scripture verse. Those on this Christian pilgrimage had brought the Spirit of the Living Lord into Israel with us. Wow, what a nugget.

Isn't that true for Christians wherever they go, allowing His Spirit in them to represent Jesus Christ? Maybe it is a question we need to ask ourselves more often.

Prayer: Father, thank You that after Jesus rose from the dead and returned to heaven, You sent as He promised, the Holy Spirit to empower us, especially to be Your witnesses. May we never take that gift for granted. Help us to yield more and more to what You want to accomplish in us and through us. Amen.

Scriptures: "But the Helper (Comforter, Advocate, Intercessor—Counselor, Strengthener, Standby), the Holy Spirit, whom the Father will send in My name [in My place, to represent Me and act on My behalf], He will teach you all things. And He will help you remember everything that I have told you." (John 14:26 ASV)

"[Jesus speaking] But you will receive power and ability when the Holy Spirit comes upon you; and you will be My witnesses [to tell people about Me] both in Jerusalem and in all Judea, and Samaria, and even to the ends of the earth." (Acts 1:6 AMP)

A Bouquet of Flowers

A famous philosopher in the Renaissance era was given accolades for his brilliant ideas and writings but he shied away for taking so much credit. He explained that he gathered flowers from other people's gardens, tied a string around them to make a bouquet and gave them to others. He was just the string, he insisted.[20]

Think about it. A bouquet is an arrangement of flowers, beautiful in color with a pleasant or sweet fragrance.

I do love that bouquet analogy. We gather flowers—ideas and concepts—from various people's gardens, put them together, make a bouquet and tie it up with a string for others.

Most of us probably do that at some time. We take. We gather. We absorb. We give.

I saw this firsthand some years ago while on a mission outreach with 15 other American women in an Indian village high in the Guatemalan mountains. Our nurses opened a temporary clinic, the teachers, a small school, and at night we preached in the church. Through interpreters we talked with their women, and one afternoon down by a lake, our women washed the feet of their women—many with babies strapped to their backs.

One morning our team leader, JoNell, and I along with our interpreter, rode in a flatbed truck as far as the dirt path led. Then we hiked the rest of the way up the mountain through coffee fields to reach the home of a pastor who asked us to come pray a blessing on his home and family. We happily entered their modest one-room dwelling with its simple tin roof and dirt floor where baby

---

[20] Arthur Gordon, *Return to Wonder*. (Nashville, TN: Broadman & Holman, 1996), 89. Illustration of Montaigne (1533-1592).

chicks scratched at our feet. Their family of four lived in one room, lighted only by a kerosene lantern—without an indoor bathroom.

I soon noticed a small coffee can holding a bouquet of stunning white calla lilies—wildflowers the pastor's wife had picked to bring beauty into her modest home.

After we had prayed for them, each of us talked excitedly through our interpreter about our Christian experiences. The Guatemalan family even sang some praise choruses in their beautiful voices. Walking back down that mountain I thought about the peace and camaraderie that I'd just experienced in that tiny home.

Whenever I recall that memorable moment, I get teary eyed because I can still picture those gorgeous lilies in a can. I thought about how flowers are sometimes used to represent Christ's love and purity. In America we often put lilies in our churches for Easter Sunday services. I heard someone say that because they grow from a bulb under earth for some time before blooming into beautiful trumpet-shaped flowers, we are reminded of His death and resurrection.

I can almost still hear those songs of praise from those precious people and remember some of the wisdom they shared with us that morning. And I will never forget.

Let's go share as that family in Guatemala did—the beauty and fragrance of a bouquet of flowers.

Prayer: Thank You, Lord, for the beauty of the earth and for the people You allow us to share our lives with. Help us to stay mindful of our influence and be good ambassadors for You. Amen.

Scriptures: "Consider the lilies, how they grow: they neither toil nor spin; and yet I say to you, even Solomon in all his glory was not arrayed like one of these." (Luke 12:27 NKJV)

"Walk into the fields and look at the wildflowers. They don't fuss with their appearance—but have you ever seen color and design quite like it? The ten best-dressed men and women in the country look shabby alongside them. If God gives such attention to the wildflowers, most of them never even seen, don't you think he'll attend to you, take pride in you, do his best for you?" (Luke 12:27-28 MSG)

Life in Lockdown During Pandemic

My doctor made a house call one day during the pandemic. We communicated face-to-face from his office to my bedroom computer. A university physician calls such online communication tools "a new technology-based clinical evaluation window." He likened it to "the use of two-way phones on opposite sides of a glass."

During the Covid pandemic, thousands of people, locked out of their downtown office building jobs, were allowed to continue working online from home or apartments while others were let go. Students from elementary through college took their classes online. Some parents of really young children had to acquire new technological skills to help their children navigate classwork on electronic tablets or computers. Some working parents, whose businesses stayed open, gave up their jobs to stay home because schools and day care centers were closed.

Still others lost their jobs because their workplace closed down or went bankrupt. Those with jobs that their state governors considered "essential" reported to work wearing masks and gloves to protect them from possible harm of catching coronavirus. With many malls shut down, people shopped online.

But nothing was usual anymore. All of us were affected. In my own family of three generations, we experienced many job and health challenges. A college student took classes from his parent's home while several others continued their office jobs working via computers from their apartments. A couple of them worked only three days a week in an "essential" store. Two close relatives continued treatments in cancer clinics while family members who drove them there had to wait in the car. Everyone has a story to tell about themselves, their relatives, or friends.

Lives were interrupted. Weddings and funerals were postponed. Seniors in Assisted Living facilities were not allowed to have family or friends visit. Isolation caused many to slip into depression. Acts of violence skyrocketed. Stores were robbed, carjackings increased, buildings and cars were burned, pastors were slapped with lawsuits when they refused to close their churches. The suicide rate went up and drugs were to blame for many as illegals brought them across our southern borders. Financial losses were felt across the marketplaces. For a while there was even a shortage of items on the grocery store shelves, like baby formula and toilet paper.

It has been predicted that it will take years to truly recover from the government-forced lockdown—and the results of vaccines which many employers forced their employees to take whether they wanted them or not. Truth is that many who took the vaccines did come down with Covid anyway. Others suffered some bad side effects.

Christians on "prayer calls" across this country prayed night and day for God's healing mercy.

Here is a prayer I wrote for my website in the summer of 2020 as a prayer for ourselves, our families, and our nation.

Prayer: Heavenly Father, during this global pandemic we come boldly to Your throne beseeching You on behalf of America, our homeland that we love. We repent of our personal and national sins, asking Your forgiveness for all the wrongs we have done. We desperately need Your divine intervention and humbly ask You to come and rescue and restore! We ask in the name of our Savior, Jesus Christ, for You to move mightily for us, our families, and our nation. Here are prayer concerns on our heart today:

- Contain and stop deadly diseases, especially Coronavirus
- Bring economic recovery for businesses, families, nation

- Restore jobs to the unemployed
- Provide safety in streets, workplaces, homes, schools, etc.
- Guard us from those seeking to harm and instill fear
- Grant wisdom to the President, Congress, state governors, city mayors, judges, and all civic leaders throughout America
- Protect our intelligence community, military, law enforcement
- Convict the mass media to be accurate when reporting news
- Heal the sick and suffering (name those you know)
- Comfort those grieving or depressed
- Guide voters to elect candidates with integrity and godly principles
- Let God's destiny for America be fulfilled
- Draw thousands to Christ with an outpouring of the Holy Spirit
- Prompt pastors to lead congregations to pray regularly for our nation
- Remove fear, anxiety, panic
- Out of chaos, restore order, justice
- Out of hopelessness, bring hope
- Out of fear, give peace and calm
- Out of hardships, rescue
- Out of doubt, renew faith

We ask this in the name of our Savior, Jesus. Amen.

Scriptures: "He who dwells in the secret place of the Most High shall remain stable and fixed under the shadow of the Almighty [Whose power no foe an withstand]. I will say of the Lord, He is my refuge and my fortress, my God, on Him I lean and rely and confidently trust." (Psalm 91:1 AMP)

"And they were at their wits' end. Then they cried to the Lord in their trouble, And He brought them out of their distresses. He caused the storm to be still." (Psalm 107:27b-29 NASB)

Visual Reminders Help Us Focus

Visual reminders can help us stay focused on our prayer concerns and our personal mission. At least it does for me.

The walls around my writing desk are covered with a Prayer Board of pictures of people I pray for; maps of the world, USA, and Israel; and a small USA flag. Quotes of unique meaning to me are also posted.

I hope you too have a specific spot to express your special interests, helping you stay motivated, inspired, and prayerful. Here are some of my "wall sayings."

Quotes N' Notes on Quin's Writing Office Wall

"O magnify the LORD with me and let us exalt His name together." (Psalm 34:3 NASB)

"The LORD will fulfill His purpose for me." (Psalm 138:8)

"My Boss Is a Jewish Carpenter."—poster

"Write the vision and make it plain upon tablets." (Habakkuk 2:2 KJV)

"Writing is what I do. I have to do it."—James A. Michener

"Expect great things from God. Attempt great things for God."

—William Carey, 1792

"Don't tell God how big your mountain is. Tell your mountain how big your God is."—Wayne Meyers

"Lord, prepare me for what You have prepared for me."—Corrie ten Boom

"Live the legacy you want to leave. Legacy lives on in people, and people live on after you are gone."—John C. Maxwell

"To whom much is given, much will be required." (Luke 12:48 NKJV)

"You Can Make a Difference."—poster

"I wonder what's going to happen exciting today?"—Piglet to Winnie the Pooh

A Prayer for Right Things

"Dear Father, in the name of Jesus Christ, I pray for the right ideas to come to me in perfect sequence and in perfect order, and in the right time and in the right way. I pray for my actual needs to be met by the right supply in the right way and at the right time. I pray for my will to be completely and utterly Your will. I pray that You, O Father, will open the door to the right work that will enable me to make my finest contribution to mankind. Amen." (See Scriptures: Mark 11:24; 1 John 5:15) Adapted from Glenn Clark, *I Will Lift Up Mine Eyes*, 1937.

My Bean Patch Prayer Board

For several decades now my Prayer Board has helped me remember all those for whom I have committed to pray for on a regular basis—to defend my bean patch. (See 2 Samuel 23:11-12.) On a simple corkboard posted near my desk I have tacked photos of family and friends. Among them are pastors, businessmen and women, homemakers, moms, singles, students, retirees, and widows. Some photos include entire families.

First, I pray for them to experience God's:

- Presence (Psalm 16: 11; 31:20; 41:12; 51:10-12)
- Protection (Psalm 5:11; 72:12-14; 91:14-16; 121:7-8)
- Provision (Joshua 2:8-9; Psalm 106:4-5; 128:1-2; Philippians 4:19)
- Peace (Psalm 4:8; 29:11; 122:7-9; 147:14)
- Precious promises to be fulfilled (2 Corinthians 1:20; 2:14; 2 Peter 1:4)

Next, I pray specifically for situations I know about which may include asking God for them to:

- Have discernment and wisdom and not be deceived in decisions facing them.
- Make wise choices financially and morally.
- Have favor in the marketplace, job, business, etc.
- Cast their cares, worries, anxieties on the Lord, trusting Him.
- Have the right people come into their life at the right time.
- Have a positive influence as they use their talents and skills.
- Experience God's healing/comforting touch (for those who need it).[21]

Some of those individuals I pray for also intercede for me from time to time. Emails, texts, and phone calls are fast ways for us to relay requests. Notes from friends pictured on my board have assured me that our prayer efforts are worthwhile. You may want to create your own unique photo board. And enjoy a blessed experience too.

Be Hospitable—No Grumbling

Be hospitable without complaint—without grumbling? That's what the Apostle Peter told the early Christians. But sometimes it seems hard. At least it did for me when I received a phone call from a stranger that late afternoon when our children were still young.

Usually, I was open to guests for a meal or overnight stays but not this evening. My husband and three children would soon be ready

---

[21] Quin Sherrer and Ruthanne Garlock, *A Woman's Guide to Spiritual Warfare*. (Bloomington, MN: Chosen Books, 2017), 224-225.

for supper, and I had an article to finish to meet my editor's deadline. Then the stranger called.

"Hi, this is Sue. We are vacationing in Florida and want to see you and your husband. Can you meet us at McDonalds and let us follow to your house?"

"How will I know you?" I asked.

"There are four of us in a yellow Cadillac with Texas license plates," she replied.

Thirty minutes later as we sat in our living room sipping iced tea, I studied Sue's face. She must be my husband's cousin, I decided. Blond, blue-eyed like his other relatives. As she talked, she seemed to know so much about us—where my husband worked, what grade our children were in, and that I was a newspaper writer.

When my husband walked in from work some moments later and saw the four guests, he arched his eyebrows at me. He didn't know them either? But they talked nonstop about people in his Texas hometown.

When the smell of chili simmering on the stove wafted into the room, Sue hinted that it must really taste good. I invited them to stay for supper. I ran to the kitchen and dumped three more cans of beans into the chili pot and made a huge, tossed salad. When my mother and children joined us, we had ten around our dining table that night.

After our meal, they moved back into the living room and began chatting once again. I realized from their talk they might be staying a lot longer. By now I was getting irritated. Sue finally asked my husband to help them find some fruit to take home. He took them to my mother's backyard to pick oranges and grapefruit. In the meantime, I cleaned up and pondered what I'd do if they really wanted to stay longer.

After a while my husband walked into the house alone. "They decided to drive a few more hours down the road and then stop at a motel," he explained.

"Who were those people? Rather, who was that Sue who knew all about us?" I asked.

"That was my mother's hairdresser," he said, laughing. "Don't you women tell your hairdresser everything? I guess Mom talked about us so much every week, Sue became very familiar with our family. The others were just her friends."

"Her hairdresser?" I said, baffled and unsure how to digest this bit of information.

After I crawled into bed that night, I pondered the incident. Now that I knew who Sue was, I began to think through the evening with greater clarity. And with great remorse for my rotten attitude.

For years my elderly mother-in-law had not been able to comb her hair properly with her crippled, gnarled, arthritic hands. In a sense Sue had been hospitable to her in a way that I couldn't since we lived over 800 miles away. Besides that, Sue had to listen to stories about us for hours—poor woman.

It was as if the Lord spoke to me: "Are three hours of your time and four bowls of chili given to strangers such a big sacrifice? Didn't I promise that if you gave even a cup of cold water in Jesus' name, you'd be rewarded?" Yes, I agreed. I asked God to forgive me for my wrong attitude toward this disruption. Then I thanked Him for forgiving me.[22]

The next morning, I was at the typewriter before daybreak, finishing my newspaper article—with a happier attitude and a new day of possibilities facing me. I am so glad He forgives us.

---

[22] Excerpted in part from *The Warm and Welcome Home* by Quin Sherrer, (Ventura, CA: Regal Books, 2004,) 81-82.

And I am glad that I was able to be hospitable on later occasions even when it seemed untimely and inconvenient.

Prayer: Lord, thank You for forgiving us and giving us opportunities to change—in attitude and actions. Thank You for the Holy Spirit to guide and teach us. Thank You for Jesus and His sacrifice for our sins. In His name I pray. Amen.

Scripture: "Be hospitable to one another without grumbling. As each one has received a gift, minister to one another as good stewards of the manifold grace of God." (1 Peter 4:2-10 NKJV)

Prayer Answers with Angelic Help

Sometimes when God answers prayer, I believe He has angels working to help with the right outcome. The Bible records many angelic encounters. He even says, "See, I am sending an angel to guard you along the way" (Exodus 23:20).

On a Friday afternoon several decades ago my prayer partner friend Lib and I were driving north from Miami back to our home in Titusville, Florida, my car loaded with houseplants my aunt had given us. We still had 100 miles to go.

That same afternoon my husband, LeRoy, was driving the same four-lane freeway, but in the opposite direction, with our pastor, Peter Lord, and several other men going south for a weekend Christian retreat.

"We might see their recreational vehicle whiz by on this busy divided highway, so let's keep an eye out for them," I told Lib. Highly unlikely I decided as I kept driving.

A few minutes later I glanced across the freeway and saw a Winnebago RV rolling south.

"Look Lib. LeRoy is probably driving that RV. But black smoke is pouring out of the back end. That vehicle is in trouble. There's no way we can go after them, not knowing how far it is to the next turn around," I said.

PONDERING MY JOURNEY

"Let's ask God to give them wisdom and to send angels to protect them," I added. So we prayed, telling God we trusted Him to send whatever help the driver needed—including angels. I felt at peace as we drove toward home, and we continued to pray but without anxiety.

Three days later, as soon as LeRoy walked in the door from the retreat, he gave me a hug and said, "Hey, we must have had an angel or two holding us up for some miles on our way down to the retreat ranch."

"I know," I replied. "Lib and I prayed and asked the Lord to surround you with angels."

"Really?" he asked. He went on with his story.

"I was driving the RV when I sensed I was losing control over the steering. I told the men I was stopping the Winnebago to go check it out. I pulled over and they got out. I drove forward, and the guys who were looking underneath said everything looked okay. Then I told them to stand clear so I could back up. When I put the RV in reverse and released the brake, the right front wheel assembly, including the axle, twisted off. The vehicle fell on top of the wheel. We had to get a wrecker and call for our friend to bring us a car so we could go to the retreat in time for supper."

None of the men had seen the smoke bellowing out. None suspected trouble. But my husband, a mechanical engineer, knew from the way the vehicle steered that something was wrong. God does intervene.

Had the prayers Lib and I prayed been the connecting link? We believed God sent angels to hold that car up until my husband could safely stop it before they had an accident. Though we have no proof.[23]

---

[23] Quin Sherrer, *Miracles Happen When You Pray*. (Carmel, NY: Guideposts Publishers, 1997) 107-108.

Years later when we lived in Colorado Springs, I made it a habit to always ask God to put angels on my car for protection when I was going to be maneuvering through traffic. One day when doing some errands, I stopped for a red light. When it turned green, I proceeded to drive forward. But an elderly driver in a larger car, coming in the opposite direction, plowed into my car. I kept stomping on the brakes, and finally came to a stop just inches from a fuel tank at a service station.

An off-duty fireman was the first person to get to me. He asked if I was alright. I said, "I asked God to put angels on my car." He looked at how close I had come to hitting the fuel tank, then said, "Lady, you may have squashed a couple of angels in stopping this car."

God's angels are present even when we don't see them. And God still answers prayer in His own way and timing. And we praise Him when we see a miracle, even when we don't know all the particulars of how He did it.

Today I pray Psalm 91 daily, and I thank Him in advance for protection for the day. "For He shall give His angels charge over you, to keep you in all your ways. In their hands they shall bear you up." (Psalm 91:11-12 NKJV)

Have you experienced a miracle you can share with others? It may build their faith!

Prayer: Thank You, Lord, for rescuing us in impossible and dangerous situations—and for sending angelic help when we need it. Thank You too for the Holy Spirit who often alerts us how to pray. Amen.

Scripture: "The angel of the Lord encamps around those who fear him, and He delivers them." (Psalm 34:7)

Speak Words of Hope

Ever felt sucker-punched? Needed a rope of hope? I did when I discovered the tumor. Breast cancer at age 84. Following surgery, the doctor recommended 33 radiation treatments. I reluctantly agreed.

A few months earlier I had jotted in my journal two sentences from a Christian speaker: "When you feel discouraged or weary in the fight, declare to your situation what you know to be true about God. Speak just one word of encouragement and hope."

During my early morning 15-mile drive to the clinic, I listened to hymns. Then while sitting in the parking lot, I asked Him for a specific word for the day. Minutes later, dressed in my pink gown, and just before entering the radiation room, I'd say to the three therapists: "The word for today is "____" followed by just one word:

Hope. Trust. Comfort. Favor. Healing. Compassion. Peace. Mercy. Strength. Courage. Faithfulness. Deliverer. Lovingkindness. Helper. Jesus. One particularly rough day it was three words for me: Be not anxious.

Some days even before I spoke, one of my compassionate therapists, would ask, "What's your word today?" One morning she said, "I needed that." Sometimes a waiting patient would ask me also for "the word." On my final day, I shouted JOY as I rang the celebration bell. The last of my faith words! Words of encouragement and hope I knew to be true about God for me in my situation.

Friends graciously provided me with prayer coverage. And I kept my hope grounded in my heavenly Father's watchcare. While "hope" has several definitions in Hebrew, the original meaning was "to stretch like a rope."

While I originally thought the "word" each day was to encourage me, it also encouraged others. But I got a bonus of encouragement myself from a virtual stranger.

I had finished my eighth radiation treatment and was beginning to burn. On my website that day was a message from a man who asked me to call because we sat next to each other on an airplane some 20 years earlier and he was suddenly thinking about me. As we finally talked, he explained that he was about to drop out of medical school that day but my pep talk on the plane encouraged him not to quit. Suddenly now he was wondering how I was. I told him the radiation burn was bothering me.

Three days later I received a box from him containing special cream to apply before and after radiation treatments to prevent burns. What a surprise! I had encouraged this future doctor. In turn he was now encouraging me—20 years later. I later wrote this encounter for a magazine under "God's Mysterious Ways."

Don't we all need hope? Encouragement? Especially in our difficult seasons. We can find it in the Bible as well as through other people. I like this Scripture, "encourage one another daily" (Hebrews 3:13).

Prayer: Dear Lord, thank You for Your Word which offers us great encouragement and hope. Thank You too for all the medical specialists who use their skills to help us fight disease. Bless them and our faithful friends who intercede for us in prayer. Thank You for being our ultimate Healer and Restorer of our bodies and souls. I pray in Jesus' name. Amen.

Scripture: "The Lord will keep your going out and your coming in from this time forth." (Psalm 121:8 AMP)

Let's Laugh More

Laughter. When was the last time you had a good laugh? When you gave way to a deep emotion which seemed to roll out of your belly—a pleasant sound, that expressed happiness, merriment, or amusement?

To start the new year off I was given a big standing wooden sign: LAUGHTER. It's now on my bookshelf staring down at me, encouraging me to take time to laugh at least once today.

PONDERING MY JOURNEY

The Bible has more than 30 references to laugh. One Scripture says there is "a time to weep and a time to laugh, a time to mourn and a time to dance" (Ecclesiastes 3:6). "He will yet fill your mouth with laughter and your lips with shouts of joy" (Job 8:21).

The Proverbs woman is described as being "clothed with strength and dignity; she can laugh at the days to come" (Proverbs 31:25).

And even this powerful one, "He who sits in the heavens shall laugh; The Lord shall hold them in derision" (Psalm 2:4).

To turn my tickle box upside down when I know I need to laugh, I try to (1) recall a funny incident I saw; or (2) something amusing I read; or (3) a hilarious story someone told me; or (4) watch a humorous video.

The Scripture that says a merry heart does good like medicine is medically true. Specialists say laughter has a good effect on heart function—it dilates blood vessels, increases muscle tone, and even increases pain tolerance. Laughter also has the potential to significantly affect the quality of our work lives. Humor helps relieve tension, reassures people, and draws them together.[24]

The gravestone of a married couple buried in our local cemetery says boldly: "We Had Fun." I laugh while wondering about all the fun they enjoyed.

Not long ago my daughter and I were sitting at a restaurant table catching up on what had happened since she had moved. We were chatting away. An elderly woman dining across from us, said a few things to us. We nodded and smiled, acknowledging her comments. But when she finished, she came and stood by our table and asked, "Do you know who I am?"

Embarrassed, I answered honestly, "Sorry, but I don't." She proceeded to tell us she was from California and had been a dance

---

[24] https://www.va.gov/WHOLEHEALTHLIBRARY/tools/healing-benefits-humor-laughter.asp

instructor for a large portion of her life. Then to my utter surprise I watched as she announced, "I am Mrs. Swivel Hips."

She began to swivel her hips and do a dance around our table, one time, two times, three times. Then she was off, swiveling around the next table of diners—dancing all the way to the cashier desk out front. The dining room exploded in laughter. A few customers even clapped for her performance.

Whenever I need a laugh, I pull Mrs. Swivel Hips and her hilarious dance routine from my memory bank—and laugh out loud once again!

Prayer: Thank You, Lord, for the gift of laughter. And for its benefits. What fun it is to laugh with family or friends—and enjoy its results. Amen.

Scriptures: "How we laughed and sang for joy. And the other nations said, 'What amazing things the Lord has done for them.'" (Psalm 126:2 TLB)

"A merry heart doeth good like a medicine: but a broken spirit drieth the bones." (Proverbs 17:22 KJV)

Part Eight: Book Writing—Work But Fun

While pondering ... I realized I have been writing books for 38 years and have had the privilege of publishing with seven different American publishers, not counting those overseas. (I've been writing magazine articles for over 50 years.)

How did I start writing books with co-writer Ruthanne Garlock—20 co-authored books with her? That's a question I am often asked.

I had been writing articles for *Aglow Magazine* for several years and their audience of women were experiencing the move of the Holy Spirit and wanted teaching tools on prayer.

So, my very first book, *How to Pray for Your Children*, was published by Women's Aglow in 1986. (I later wrote an updated version, *A Mother's Guide to Praying for Your Children* for Chosen.)

The original book became well-known among Aglow fellowship groups because moms wanted to know how to pray more effectively for their children. As a result of that little book with the bright green cover, I was invited to speak often, travelling across the nation. However, Aglow Publications asked me to write a book sequel, but I had only gotten it half finished.

I was speaking on praying for your children at a retreat in the hill country of Texas when Ruthanne Garlock brought her mother and prayer partner to hear me. I had met Ruthanne briefly a few years earlier when she was the director of a Christian Writing Conference on Christ for the Nations campus in Dallas where her husband John was a Bible instructor. Jamie Buckingham, my writing mentor, had suggested I attend that Writers Conference because of the outstanding Christian authors who would be teaching. If I hadn't gone, I might never have met Ruthanne.

Ruthanne came to the seminar on praying for children and heard me say I was trying to finish writing another book on prayer for Aglow Publications. She asked me a pointed question. "You have your manuscript in the trunk of your car, don't you?" Yes, I did. I had driven all the way from Florida to the Texas hills, thinking I might have time to work on it between teaching sessions. "Go get it and let me read it," she said.

She took my half-written manuscript to her room where her prayer partner and her mother joined her in praying. Should she be the writer to help me finish it? Yes, she was.

Not only did we finish that Aglow book but then Servant Publications called me and asked if we would write a book for them on praying for families. And that started a series of many books for them followed by Regal (Gospel Light), Zondervan, Chosen (Baker Book Group), Spanish House, and others.

We made a good team as Ruthanne had a degree in Bible and religious education from Central Bible College and I had a degree in journalism from Florida State University. We were also blessed with great editors.

Ruthanne and I continued to write books together—though she lived in Texas while I lived in three different states while we co-wrote. I would usually go to her house for our final week of writing. How great it is now to use email for sending manuscripts back and forth. In our earlier book writing days, we stood in line at a post office to get our thick manuscript stamped with the date we were mailing it to our publisher—proving we made their deadline.

But I was also busy writing eleven books on my own in-between writing with Ruthanne and I was travelling to speak and so was she.

One of our most rushed but rewarding book projects happened right after the September 2001 catastrophe at the Twin Towers, the Pentagon, and a field in Pennsylvania, when almost 3,000 people lost their lives. Ruthanne and I were asked to write a book that would help people pray for our grieving nation. The catch was we had three weeks to do it. But with God's help and very little sleep, we did it!

The book *God Be With Us: A Daily Guide to Praying for Our Nation* was nominated by the Evangelical Christian Publishers Association for the 2002 Gold Medallion award in the devotional category. Ruthanne and I were honored to receive that award at the Christian Booksellers Convention. Several congressmen read our book.

I was also blessed to receive the Writer of the Year award at the Florida Writers In Touch event. The Guideposts Magazine Writers Workshop contest win allowed me to study under some well-known Christian authors for a week in Rye, New York.

Writing books opened the door for interviews on radio and television as well as speaking invitations on those book topics. I was always filled with gratitude for each opportunity to minister and encourage others.

I have been especially happy that our books have reached hundreds in other countries because they were translated into about 15 foreign languages including Portuguese, Spanish, German, Korean, Chinese, Czech, and others.

I learned early on that authoring books requires lots of discipline. I found my best writing time was early morning, sometimes even

PONDERING MY JOURNEY

5:00 a.m. when I would often get up, grab a mug of coffee, and begin to peck away on my typewriter keyboard. Thankfully computers became affordable. I still find mornings are my best creative times for writing blogs for my website. And yes, I am still writing them at 90.

Soon after the first edition of *A Woman's Guide to Spiritual Warfare* was released in 1991, it hit the top-selling list for Christian books in the spiritual warfare category and kept that rating for six years. We revised it several times, and it continues to be our most popular one. Comments still come to us from women and men who got their copy online or from a book rack in a grocery store, bookstore, airport, or military base.

One publisher asked us to write "guides for Christian women" and we wrote these: *A Woman's Guide to Breaking Bondages; A*

Woman's Guide to Getting Through Tough Times; A Woman's Guide to Spirit-Filled Living; A Woman's Guide to Spiritual Warfare. (See others listed in back of this book.)

After Zondervan published my book *Miracles Happen When You Pray*, I was thrilled when Guideposts republished it as a hardback for their yearly book club edition. Of all the books I've written, it remains my favorite because I had the privilege to interview people from across this country who told me their miracle stories, which honored our loving God. After my husband died, I wrote *Hope for a Widow's Heart* for Authentic Publishers. Though some of the earlier books are out of print, many are still available as e-books and used copies are available at online outlets.

I am forever thankful to God for the privilege I have had to write. And for the wonderful people who have read those books. I am also grateful to those who played a part in taking what I wrote on paper and getting it into the hands of those who wanted or needed those books—agents, publishers, copyreaders, editors, marketing people, bookstore managers, and an assortment of others. I am appreciative too for those involved in the radio and television programs who helped their audiences know about our books.

Prayer: Lord, thank You for the gift of writing. Bless all those who have been on this journey with me—readers and those who helped get my words into print. Please bless them everyone. May the words that I wrote help bring others closer to our Savior. I ask in the name of Jesus. Amen.

Scriptures: "This is what the Lord, the God of Israel, says: 'Write in a book all the words I have spoken to you.'" (Jeremiah 30:2)

"And then God answered: 'Write this. Write what you see. Write it out in big block letters so that it can be read on the run.'" (Habakkuk 2:2 MSG)

Part Nine: World Adventures

What an awesome journey I have had, as I mentioned earlier—travelling to 26 nations, speaking to audiences in 12 of them and in most of the States. I am so grateful for these opportunities to travel on ministry trips, writing assignments and overseas tours.

I count it a privilege to have preached in Russia, Japan, Argentina, Germany, Korea, Belgium, Holland, Denmark, Canada, Mexico, Guatemala, Hawaii, Puerto Rico, as well as in the States.

Here are a few of my adventure memories—though some happened so long ago, remembering details is not easy now.

Germany. It was October 1983. I had been taking care of my mother for 13 months during her battle with cancer. When she left for heaven, I was physically exhausted. Her prayer partner, JoAnne Bailey, was still living in Wiesbaden, Germany where her husband was a doctor in the Air Force. She begged me to come there for some refreshing. Our mutual friend, Beth Alves from Texas, was staying with her and would be the conference speaker for the upcoming Aglow Conference for American military wives. I had not seen any of them in a long time, so Germany here I come. Our longtime friend Tommie Woods agreed to go with me.

Now the four of us were enroute to Berchesgarten to attend the Aglow conference. I especially recall our harrowing ride to the General Walker Hotel in a taxi around the hairpin curves—for we were in the third highest mountain range in Germany. I was sitting in the front with the driver and when I looked out the window to the deep, deep valley below, I lost it and so did my bladder! Those friends riding in the backseat laughed and never let me forget it.

I was asked to write an article about the conference for Aglow Magazine and to do that I had to borrow the hotel typewriter and use it at night in a basement room. I was told that this was the same room where Adolf Hitler wrote some of his most evil works. (His vacation home, "Eagle's Nest" is nearby.) As I typed, Tommie walked the floor, praying for me to be able to hit the right letters on that typewriter with all its unfamiliar German symbols. Well, I finished the article, mailed it to Seattle and it arrived for publication before we got back to the States.

One side trip Tommie and I took together was to nearby Salzburg, Austria just for a day. The baroque architecture was spectacular, but we also toured the museum of Wolfgang Mozart, the city's most famous son. On the way we passed the "mansion" where the "Sound of Music" movie was made about the Von Trapp family's life during the early days of World War II.

For the next two weeks JoAnne took Tommie, Beth, and me on some wonderful trips to Frankfort, Heidelberg, and other cities to visit old castles, and to see quaint villages.

But our trip to Darmstadt was a highlight. Here the Sisters of Mary had built a retreat and convent (Lutheran primarily) from the ruins of the war. Their gardens had no insects as long as there was no unforgiveness among the women who lived there, and their fruit trees were enormous (we ate from them). We attended worship services that afternoon at three o'clock, commemorating Jesus' time on the cross. We were blessed to hear these dear older ladies who had survived World War II singing praises to God. We walked the stations of the cross there, smelled the fragrance, and wept a tear or two. Sister Basilea Schlink, founder of Sisters of Mary tells her personal story in *A Foretaste of Heaven*. They have a sisterhood in Phoenix, which I have also seen, and one on Mount of Olives in Israel.

Four friends meet in Phoenix at a Christian women's conference where Quin taught a writer's workshop—Kerry, Quin, JoNell, and Mary Jo.

Russia. I had wanted to visit Russia for some time and carried a prayer burden for the nation. So many needed to know Jesus as Savior. Thousands had suffered through Stalin's purges.

Finally in the 1990s, after the Cold War ended, I was going as co-leader with Barbara (Bobbye) Byerly, U.S. Aglow president, accompanying 20 Aglow women on a short-term mission trip.

We flew into St. Petersburg from New York for our first stop off. There we spent a half day at the magnificent Hermitage Museum—once known as the Winter Palace. Of all the famous art works, I was so touched by the 300-year-old painting by Rembrandt of "The Prodigal Son." We visited a Russian Orthodox Church which had been used by Stalin's minions to make statues of him. We stood during this church service in the massive building that was attended mostly by a small gathering of older women, the faithful intercessors during the days when communism forbid religious services. There were no chairs or benches in these former grand cathedrals because Stalin had taken them over for other purposes. I had taken a suitcase full of Russian language Bibles, each with a concordance, which we left with a seminary in St. Petersburg. I had purchased them at the International Bible headquarters in Colorado Springs.

In the city of Novgorod, our Aglow team ministered the love of Jesus in an orphan home, a hospital for critically ill children, and another facility for recovering alcoholic women. (Two women in our group later adopted children from that orphanage.) We conducted church services that week in a rented gymnasium room where the newly established Vineyard Church congregation usually met. As I preached, through an interpreter, I stood on a chair so the audience could see me better, especially those standing in the hallways who could not get into the overcrowded room. I left one suitcase of medicines donated by a doctor in our Colorado Springs church for the doctor/pastor of this church in Novgorod. One problem while there was trying to find vending machines with enough bottled water for our group.

We had a scary moment one afternoon when Barbara and I were in our hotel room and Russian planes making earsplitting noise flew so low we were concerned as we watched from our windows. Our interpreter ran to knock on our door and yelled, "Dear ladies, it is just military practice. Practice. Don't be afraid," he assured us.

The scenery from a 17-hour train ride through Russia was beautiful except when I observed the peasant women out farming—their circumstances were so sad. The bathrooms and berths on that train were unbelievably bad. We prayed hard for the Lord to protect us from the men banging on our berth door. They finally left without breaking in. We had been warned to be alert for robbers on train rides.

In Moscow's Red Square on an early Sunday morning, we had an impromptu worship service. Afterwards, I walked over to the building holding the mausoleum with the body of one-time communist leader Vladimir Lenin and thanked God that communism was no longer preeminent in this nation. I shouted at the top of my lungs, "Lenin is dead, but Jesus Christ is alive!" We Americans were the only people I observed in Red Square that morning—at a site where military troops and tanks used to roll through in a big demonstration of power. Moscow was our last stop after almost two weeks of ministry in Russia. With no ministry planned for our two-day stay, we attended a circus, a magnificent ballet performance, and made a visit to a McDonald's restaurant for a hamburger.

Some of the sights in Moscow were breathtaking such as St. Basil's Cathedral. We enjoyed as many tourist sites as we could manage. Then we flew back to New York.

Japan. I initially went to Japan to be keynote speaker for two retreats for wives of American servicemen. I was so happy that Cindy Edwards travelled with me from Colorado to play the piano and sing, providing worship music wherever I spoke.

How can I forget the night we slept on a mat on the floor in a Japanese home as guests of a gracious host family? The room was so small we could not even get a suitcase in it—as both Cindy and I shared a mat. We were glad they had an American style toilet though! So pleased that I had this great experience in a real Japanese home.

I felt privileged to be retreat speaker for the American women—Protestant Women of the Chapel—whose husbands were military servicemen stationed there. I did the retreat on one military base one weekend. And then we travelled to the other end of the island where the women from that base held the retreat in a Japanese fitness camp. At night the women all slept on the floor in one big room. But they provided Cindy and me with Army cots in a private room, which was a nice gesture. The American women had to do kitchen duty after every meal and were required to show up outdoors for the morning calisthenics.

PONDERING MY JOURNEY

One night between these two retreats, Cindy and I boarded a plane in Tokyo to go to another island. The next day I spoke to the Aglow women through a wonderful interpreter. Many years later when Dutch Sheets used one of my blogs on his *Give Him 15* posts, that interpreter read it in Japan and contacted me. Having a good interpreter when one speaks in another nation is a blessing, and I speak from experience.

On our way to downtown Tokyo, Cindy and I rode in a very clean and packed train. A uniformed man on the platform had pushed us onto the train to pack it as tightly as possible with passengers and it was full of businessmen and women. Cindy began to sing, and they seemed to enjoy it. She even sang, "Oh, the Blood of Jesus."

At the Tokyo Aglow meeting, many of the women ate their sack lunches while I spoke and most also stayed for prayer afterwards. When the Holy Spirit touched them, they "rested" on the floor.

Another highlight in Japan was May 1st on a U.S. military base as we participated in a National Day of Prayer for America ceremony. A large group gathered around 50 American flags that snapped in the high wind. I was a visitor, just one in the crowd composed of members of a military band, choirs, school children, and servicemen and women with their families who met to pray for our nation. As we sang, "God bless America, land that I love," I felt deep gratitude to God for my homeland and for the men and women who serve in the military. As I approached the platform to give the history of the National Day of Prayer, I felt privileged to participate in this service. Yet it was the day before they observed this event in the United States due to time zone differences.

Other Adventures

Argentina. In Buenos Aires, in the early 1990s, I sat in a massive sports stadium, praising God with Christians from other nationalities while my friend Cindy Jacobs preached. I was one of the intercessors attending this massive worship service but about 100 of us Americans were participating in smaller meetings spearheaded by Dr. C. Peter Wagner as we listened and learned from the Argentine evangelists who had been experiencing massive revivals. We visited some of the big Christian gatherings where the Holy Spirit outpourings were taking place. I was impressed that they had revival meetings in one tent and those who got "saved" then went to the next tent for "deliverance" ministry. I got to minister during this trip also.

Belgium. After I had spoken to Aglow fellowship, we had to exit out a back way because there were riots and policemen on horseback who were trying to control the crowds because something about political riots were taking place.

Holland. We also traveled to Holland where I spoke and saw places significant in the life of evangelist Corrie ten Boom including the prison where Corrie and her family were first locked up after being arrested for hiding Jews. Many of the prisoners died later in the Nazi German prison camp, including Corrie's sister, Betsie, and their father. But Corrie, in her early 50s survived and became an evangelistic *"Tramp for the Lord"* until her death at 91 in California. (I had met her when Jamie Buckingham was writing a book for her with that same title.)

Denmark. In Copenhagen, the hotel banquet room was packed while I preached. I spent several days with my daughter Sherry who lived there. She and I took a boat to Sweden for the day—a fun time.

Korea. I later travelled with JoAnne Bailey to Seoul, where we attended Yoido Full Gospel Church, which had the largest membership of any Christian church in the world, founded by Dr. David Yonggi Cho. (Today it is said to have 480,000 members.) I was touched when the entire congregation prayed aloud when a bell rang and stopped when the next bell rang out. What a majestic sound with thousands praying at the same time. We attended just one of their many services that Sunday.

PONDERING MY JOURNEY

We spent a week in Korea at a prayer conference at the famous Methodist Prayer Mountain with members of our American team—Chuck Pierce, Cindy Jacobs, Peter Wagner, Jane Hansen, and others. JoAnne and I were on the intercessory team covering the key speakers from Christian ministries conducting the conference. Intercessors kept prayer going 24 hours, taking turns in shifts. They brought in Army cots for us to sleep on after Dr. Wagner told the management Americans were not used to sleeping on the floor. JoAnne's husband called me to tell JoAnne that her dad had died in South Carolina, so we had a short memorial service, comforting her.

Canada. In Canada I was blessed to be keynote speaker at an Aglow Regional Conference attended by 300 women. We had anointed times of worship, sharing, and fellowshipping. During the last session of this three-day event, there was an amazing outpouring of the Spirit. Musicians led the audience to sing, "Holy Spirit, You are welcome in this place" repeatedly. Many women who stood under one of the prayer shawls were so touched by the Holy Spirit they were soon resting on the floor.

In Winnipeg I was a speaker along with one of Pat Boone's daughters. She and I even did a Christian radio interview together too.

Other Worldwide Trips with Husband

Italy. Gondola rides down the canals of Venice, glassblowers, the magnificent St. Marks Basilica. In Rome meandering through the catacombs where early Christians worshiped in secret and the Colosseum where some were martyred. The Pantheon, Sistine Chapel, St. Peter's Cathedral. In Florence at the Medici Chapel admiring Michelangelo's masterpieces.

France. Walking the streets of Paris in the rain with friends while LeRoy was in bed at the hotel with a cold the first day. Notre Dame, Eiffel Tower, Napoleon's Tomb, flea markets.

Zurich, Switzerland. Spending the night in a hotel so high up in the Alps, we had to take a train to get there.

London. Big Ben, Buckingham Palace, St. Paul's Cathedral, Hyde Park. Shopping at Harrods, with a massive range of departments. Impressed with Westminster Abbey where many royal weddings and funerals have taken place but drawn so much to the famous buried there, especially to David Livingstone's tomb below the church floor.

Rotterdam, Amsterdam; Brussels, Lucerne, Innsbruck. Some exciting weeks on a tour.

Israel. The first time I went was Christmas week in 1972 with my 13-year-old Quinett to walk where Jesus walked. Watching her ride off on a camel with a Bedouin guide was fine, until I lost sight of her momentarily and it frightened me. Visiting Bethlehem and the spot where supposedly Jesus was born during the week of Christmas was a dream come true. We also got to visit Hebron and the cave holding the tombs of Abraham, Sarah, Isaac, Jacob, and Leah (now off-limits to tourists). Highlight of that trip was getting baptized in same river as Jesus in the cold River Jordan on January 1, 1973, very early in the morning and having to change clothes on the bus.

Then the next trip to Israel was years later when LeRoy and I travelled with a group from Jamie Buckingham's church. We stayed primarily in a Jerusalem hotel, but spent one night in a kibbutz, took a boat ride on the Sea of Galilee, saw Bethlehem, Jericho, Masada, Capernaum, and other ancient Jewish and Christian sites. I was so glad for the opportunity to pray for our families at the Western Wall with friends Laura Watson and Hilda Forehand who were on the trip with us.

We flew from Israel to Greece where I stood on Mars Hill like Paul, and I proclaimed a gospel message too. We saw Corinth, toured, and hiked about Athens, and walked around the Parthenon. It was my second trip to Greece as Quinett and I had gone there after our trip to Israel. She was in the eighth grade and amazed others on our tour with her knowledge of all the ancient sites we were seeing.

World's Fair. In October 1965, LeRoy and I had attended the World's Fair in Flushing Meadows, New York. The Pope visited that day too and we saw his motorcade outside our hotel window. The fair's theme was "Peace Through Understanding" dedicated to "Man's Achievement on a Shrinking Globe in an Expanding Universe" and was symbolized by a 12-story-high, stainless-steel model of the earth called the Unisphere.

My Experiences

There were special times in my life when I felt engulfed by God's presence. Such precious times when the Holy Spirit was ministering to me, and I was enjoying the fellowship of the Lord. I could relate to the Psalmist who said, "In Your presence is fullness of joy" (Psalm 16:11 NKJV).

In the latter 1990s a friend and I went to a Catch The Fire Conference at the Airport Vineyard Church in Toronto. John and Carol Arnott were the lead pastors, but we heard other anointed speakers, including a Baptist pastor I knew from Florida. For three days I spent some prayer time on the carpet, laughed a bit, and wept as I experienced encounters with the Holy Spirit that impacted me greatly.

We sat in a packed auditorium where there was powerful worship, inspirational teachings, testimonies, and even miracle healings. I talked to a lot of others there who told me how they were being renewed by soaking in God's presence. A Presbyterian elder from Australia who sat next to me laughed loud and often, explained that he felt such joy of the Lord. At the airport, the customs agent who checked me into Canada, told me people were flying in from all over the world to come to "The Toronto Blessing." (Actually, services were held there every night but Mondays for 12 straight years.)

Even now I read posts from people who criticize those meetings where there were signs and wonders. But I know I had a spiritual renewal there and so did a lot of others.

One Sunday I was the guest speaker in a Michigan Assembly of God Church for their two morning services. Among those attending the first were 20 young men from Teen Challenge, most recovering drug addicts, who were such an attentive audience. During my speech I mentioned a phrase which missionary Wayne Myers used so often: "Don't tell God how big your mountain is. Tell your mountain how big God is." I got a lot of "amens" and smiles from those men with that statement.

When the second service began, the worship leader told the congregation he wanted to introduce a new chorus. He had put to music the phrase I had used earlier, and he led them to sing, "Don't tell God how big your mountain is. Tell your mountain how big God is."

Wayne Myers would have been pleased to have heard that singing. Though he spent most of his time as a missionary in Mexico, he kept an apartment adjoining ours on the Christ for the Nations campus in Dallas. Whenever he was there, he would do some loud praying. Often when I heard him, I'd put my hands against the wall adjoining his room next door and pray in agreement with him.

In Colorado Springs, I was immensely honored to lead a prayer retreat for Mrs. James Dobson (Shirley) and her personal intercessors in September 2001 soon after America's 9/11 tragedy. She was then chairman of the National Day of Prayer in the U.S. which always meets in Washington, D.C. on the first Thursday in May. But this was just for her intercessors. We met in a home in Colorado Springs, with a beautiful view of the towering Pikes Peak, over 14,000 feet above sea level—a graphic reminder of our great Creator God. And we prayed much for our nation that day.

PONDERING MY JOURNEY

I once stood behind the pulpit in the Cane Ridge Meeting House in Kentucky, trying to imagine what it was like during those few days in August 1801 when an estimated 20,000 or more from varied cultures and economic standings showed up for what became known as the Western Great Revival. "A religious phenomenon," said one eyewitness. "Thousands were experiencing the new birth," reported another. And I prayed such a revival, another Great Awakening, would come to America again soon.

In Los Angeles, California, I stood on the platform of the Angelus Temple Church where the Pentecostal evangelist Aimee Semple McPherson held preaching and healing services in the 1920s and 1930s. Cindy Jacobs had invited me to accompany her to see where the founder of the Foursquare Churches had once ministered. I was impressed with the number of wheelchairs, crutches, and canes in the glass cases lining the hallways which were left by people who were healed by the power of God while attending services back then. I have a longing for great healing services like that to happen again.

In Montreat, North Carolina, I attended a service where Katherine Kuhlman began her preaching with the invitation, repeating over and over, "Holy Spirit, come. You are welcome here." Jamie Buckingham was the host who introduced her. Many people were healed as God touched them. Afterwards almost the entire congregation remained in their seats—the anointing of the Holy Spirit was so awesome, we couldn't walk. Later when my friends and I tried to make our way back to our dorm rooms, Dot fell to the ground, still unsteady on her feet. I went to one of Miss Kuhlman's services in Orlando another time where there were many healing miracles.

I often did freelance writing for magazines and other newspapers, even a few secular periodicals. Once in Florida I had one of my most unusual interviews for an article. I sat in the backseat of a car interviewing a U.S. presidential candidate for a newspaper assignment while he was enroute to his next campaign speaking engagement. I had only 20 minutes to do this. He held my tape recorder while I also took copious notes. Two Secret Service men accompanied us. My article was published in a newspaper with national coverage. And the candidate was elected president of the United States.

Television, Radio, and Retreats

Some of my most rewarding experiences were doing television and radio interviews on Christian channels after a new book was published. I did over 375 of these appearances, talking to audiences in places I might never go. A large portion of the radio interviews were by phone from my home, but not all.

Of course, the television interviews were onsite, and I usually flew to get there—Denver, Dallas, Albuquerque, Los Angeles, Tampa, Virginia Beach, Winnipeg, Toronto, and other cities. I was always grateful for the host and hostesses who invited me to appear. *Daystar*, *Trinity Broadcast*, *The 700 Club*, *100 Huntley Street*, *It's A New Day*, *On Main Street* among them.

September 2001 found me in Virginia Beach appearing on the television show, *The 700 Club*, founded by Pat Robertson. He and I exchanged lively conversation while the makeup artist prepared us for the camera. (He died in June 2023.) During the several times I was on their programs I enjoyed the people who worked with me as well as the students I met at the Regent University there.

Sometimes at studios the unusual happened to give us all a laugh! I was in an eastern state and scheduled to be the second television interview for the day to talk about my latest book on prayer. The guest ahead of me had a pet Vietnamese potbellied pig she was showing off—I have no idea why. But during the break as the host was hugging the miniature pig good-bye, the animal messed up her blouse. My traveling companion, JoAnne, looked at me, and laughingly said, "Hey, pigs and prayer don't go together too well." The host did a quick change of clothes, and we went on the air on time.

Teaching at an Aglow retreat on her book **How to Pray for Your Children.**

Quin as keynote speaker at Christ for the Nations for a week in Dallas.

I had the privilege of speaking in many of the States, often for week-end retreats to church women's groups, Aglow fellowships, Protestant Women of the Chapel, and sometimes to Sunday morning church congregations.

One memorable weekend in a western state in the middle of winter the Aglow retreat was attended by mainly wives of farmers and ranchers. As word spread that a blizzard was on the way some left early to try to get home to help their husbands with their livestock.

The rest of us were stranded for two more days as snow blanketed the hotel and buried the cars in the parking lot. The hotel where we held the retreat was now full of truck drivers and others who did not evacuate soon enough. The hotel was running out of food so for each meal they served what they had—and that included eggs for every meal. How strange it seemed that guests went swimming in the heated hotel pool while snow continued falling outside. When we finally got ready to leave some truck driver heroes shoveled snow off the cars so the guests could travel home. I later heard the sad news that many of the farms belonging to those families lost numerous heads of cattle during that awful storm. But thankfully all the women from our retreat arrived home safely.

Traveling to and from some of these locations was not always easy. I was stuck in Canadian airports for an entire day twice when flights were cancelled. Once I was approached by drug pushers in a hotel hallway. We had a car wreck in Kentucky. A policewoman pulled over my friend driving when we were lost, trying to find our motel in the wee hours of the morning in a North Carolina city—before GPS was available. Once at our retreat center high in the mountains, a bear had emptied the lodge's refrigerator the night before. Now those events seem trivial. The truth is the Lord took care of me, and I did not suffer harm.

PONDERING MY JOURNEY

Quin in Washington, D.C. with Cindy Jacobs, chairman of Deborah Company, praying with her for the United States at a large conference in 2019.

Speaking of television and broadcasting of gospel messages, I want to mention that once when I was a newspaper reporter near Kennedy Space Center, I did an interview with an evangelist from Timor, Indonesia. During a spiritual revival that started in 1965 he had seen miracles much like the early church—the crippled walked, the deaf heard, the mute spoke, leprosy and cancer were healed. He told me he was excited to be on hand for the launch of this satellite because when he preached now it was going to help him reach thousands in the remote communities of the Indonesian islands.

My interview with him gave me a new appreciation for my husband and all other aerospace engineers who worked to get those satellites in space. Now millions could hear the good news of the gospel and hopefully receive Jesus as their Savior around the world.

Quin at age 88, praying for the media while Florida Aglow leader Sherry Anderson moderates the Day of Prayer for the Seven Mountains of Influence.

Prayer: Lord, thank You for the airways that are now being used to preach the gospel about our Lord Jesus Christ. Thank You for those who work at these Christian stations to help get the message broadcast. Give them courage and boldness to continue to reach the masses. And give their audiences a listening ear to hear and receive the message about Jesus' love for them. Let many be swept into the Kingdom through radio and television outreach. Amen.

Scripture: "And this gospel of the kingdom will be preached in the whole world as a testimony to all nations, and then the end will come." (Matthew 24:14)

Wrong Place

My friend Ginger had driven me many long hours to reach the city where I was to speak the following day. Our hostess invited us to use the entire upstairs of their large home. That evening when I noticed the spacious bathroom had a jacuzzi, I insisted that Ginger use that one. I went down the hall into the smaller bathroom, slipped into the tub I'd filled with warm water, and began to lather on the funny smelling soap. I looked around the room more closely and realized I was in the dog's bathroom, covered with his flea soap. Grabbing Muffy's towel, I quickly made my exit. We got a laugh out of that one for days afterwards.

Surprise Airplane Encounters

Sometimes a "someone" crosses your path just once in your lifetime, but the encounter is so startling you smile years later remembering it. I had several surprising experiences on airplane trips on my way to speak. Here are a few of them.

I boarded a plane in Colorado headed to Virginia to do a television interview on my newest book. When we got off in Chicago to make connecting flights, I was surprised to see a young man about the age of my adult son who had been on my plane—waiting for me.

"Lady," he said, "We have a mutual friend."

"Well, who is it?" I asked puzzled. "You look like you are in the military."

"Yes, I am, but my friend is not. He is the Jewish Carpenter from Nazareth."

"How do you know I know Him?"

"I watched you on the plane—reading your Bible," he explained.

"Yes, I know Jesus of Nazareth, and He is more than a friend. He's my Savior. I am on my way to talk about Him on a television show. But I may miss my plane since we are running late."

He asked where I was headed, checked the overhead monitors, grabbed my carry-on bag, and yelled, "Follow me, I'll get you there." We made a mad dash on escalators, down long corridors. I almost ran every step to keep up with him.

Just as we arrived at my gate, the airline attendant announced last call for passengers to board. My "military escort" handed me my luggage, and I waved good-bye.

But I forgot to tell him about the sign in my writing office: "My Boss Is A Jewish Carpenter."

Whenever I see that sign—still there after many years and many moves—I think of the young man whose shadow fell on me that autumn morning. At the right place at the right time with a serving heart. My airport angel. He may have headed off to war after that. But someday we'll meet in heaven with our very famous "Mutual Friend." Our Savior, Jesus Christ.[25]

Another time while waiting to board an airplane, I had a lively conversation about the Lord with a professional basketball player sitting next to me. He kept talking enthusiastically about his praying grandmother. I gave him one of my books on prayer as we began to make our way onto the plane.

I took my aisle seat while he made his way further back. We'd been in the air a while when the airline attendant serving snacks whispered to me, "When I am through serving would you pray for me?"

"Of course I will. Be glad to. But why did you ask me specifically?"

"The man sitting back there is engrossed reading a book. When I asked what he was reading, he said it was about prayer and that you wrote it."

---

[25] Quin Sherrer, *Cast Your Shadow: Influence on Purpose*. (CreateSpace/Kindle, 2018) 46, 47.

PONDERING MY JOURNEY

Later she came back and knelt in the aisle beside me. It only looked like we were talking to each other—but I was talking to God, asking Him to solve her difficult situation.

Once, on a flight from Orlando to Atlanta where I had to change planes, I introduced myself to the woman sitting beside me. When I mentioned my name, she literally screamed, "You wrote that book that helped save my marriage and my children! I copied the prayers from *A Woman's Guide to Spiritual Warfare* and asked my husband to pray them aloud with me every day. Our daughter was falling into bad company. But we used these prayers and examples to give us hope. Today we are a family following the Lord and active in the church."

She gave me her phone number in case I got delayed in Atlanta and needed a place to stay overnight. For the rest of the trip, we enjoyed a great conversation, but I never saw her again. A chance meeting? No, for me it was a God-ordained encounter, a connection I needed that day.

Shortly after the September 11, 2001, terrorist attack on our nation, I was on a crowded airplane flying to Texas. Before takeoff the pilot got on the microphone and advised passengers to get acquainted with our seatmates, to share family pictures, to really get to know some facts about them. Because, he said, in these uncertain days we may need to know that information.

We were preparing for takeoff when the 50-something-year-old man seated next to me closed his cell phone and said, "Well, I just made a lot of money on that call."

I laughingly replied, "What are you doing sitting so far back in the plane beside me? Shouldn't you be in first class?"

"Overbooked," he assured me. Six others of his company men were on the plane too.

After he explained about his burn-resistant invention he was going to Texas to test, I complimented him on his sharp mind and great skills. "But we have a Creator God who gives us these ideas. I believe God inspired yours. Sounds like your invention will benefit a lot of people," I told him. This grabbed his attention, and he asked more questions. I tried to introduce him to our big God.

Between a few curse words, he told me bluntly he was not a believer, but his wife was very religious. Yet he was still shaken by the deaths of more than 20 from his New Jersey community who perished in the Twin Towers collapse. He told me stories about some of those he knew and the funerals he'd attended. I asked the proverbial question, "If you had died that day too, where would you be today?" While he didn't answer, I tried to tell him how people could have eternal life through Jesus. He just smiled and was silent awhile.

Then he reached into his wallet and showed me a half dozen pictures of his adorable five-year-old daughter, bragging about the designer clothes he had bought her. Sighing, he admitted he was so busy traveling he hardly got home to see her. I strongly encouraged him to find the time for her and his beautiful young wife because someday he would not want to live with regrets.

I won't ever know the results of our conversation that day, but I believe God had an encounter planned for both of us.

Right now, think about a coincidental meeting you may have had, a God-inspired encounter, perhaps with someone you didn't even know.

Prayer: Thank You, Father, for arranging encounters with some people with whom our lives have connected but are often unplanned. When these amazing events happen, I am surprised but most grateful. I praise You for such serendipities in my life. Thank You for our Savior in whose name I pray. Amen.

Scripture: "And be kind to one another, tenderhearted..." (Ephesians 4:32 NKJV)

PONDERING MY JOURNEY

Quote: "Every experience God gives us, every person He puts in our lives, is the perfect preparation for the future that only He can see." —Corrie ten Boom

Scotland Sights and Insights

Explore Edinburgh on our own? Our tour guide encouraged us to walk wherever we wanted to go in that ancient city one cool May afternoon. My sister and I were in Scotland in memory of our late mother who never achieved her lifelong dream to come and check out her Lamont clan.

Without guidebooks, we walked the streets near our hotel, turning slightly off Royal Mile, until we came upon a building originally built in 1622. Carving above the door read: "Feare The Lord and Depart From Evil." Another sign read, "Writers' Museum." Both signs intrigued me. We walked in, and for thirty minutes we had the museum to ourselves.[26]

The building was dedicated to three of Scotland's most famous writers—-Robert Burns (1759-1796), Sir Walter Scott (1771-1832), and Robert Lewis Stevenson (1850-1894). As a writer I was delighted by this discovery. Our mother, who won awards for reciting long poems in her high school "elocution" contests, had encouraged us as children to read and memorize some of their works.

The small museum was crammed with pictures, etchings, busts, and memorabilia of the three writers, including Bibles, pipes, and walking canes. Rare books, Burns' writing desk, first edition books, and handwritten manuscripts grabbed my attention. I could hardly contain myself.

I touched what was permitted, sat where seats were provided, and recalled as many verses from these well-known writers as I could. I tried to imagine Robert Lewis Stevenson, ranked among the 26

---

[26] http://www.cityofliterature.com/a-to-z/writers-museum-2/ accessed March 22, 2017.

most translated authors in the world, writing his famous children's poems.[27] Just that morning our tour bus stopped in front of the house where he once lived, and a little towheaded youngster came to the front window and waved at us.

When my children were young, I read them from Robert Stevenson's *A Child's Garden of Verses*, and later they read his *Treasure Island*. Robert Burns, known for his romance writing, and poems even composed the song "Auld Lang Syne." Sir Walter Scott, on the other hand, wrote novels, mysteries, poems, and was appreciated by his countrymen for keeping Scottish history alive even in his fiction.

During various seasons of my life, the writings of these three men impacted me. Now looking over their memorabilia in the museum I had a better feel for what their life and writing habits were like.

Leaving the building, my sister and I headed back toward our hotel, where we found ourselves standing in front of a picturesque townhouse built prior to 1490. The sign indicated it was where Rev. John Knox the Scottish Reformer once lived. Upon entering the museum, we were told we were fortunate because it had only reopened that day after being closed for some time. What a happy surprise.

Knox lived from 1514 to 1572 and was known for spearheading the Protestant Reformation of Scotland and influencing the early Presbyterians from his pulpit in St. Giles Cathedral which was nearby. This was, however, not his residence the entire time he lived in Edinburgh.

Passionate in his desire for his nation's people to have a personal relationship with Christ, Knox prayed often, "Give me Scotland, or I die." When copies of Tyndale's translation of the Bible were smuggled into Scotland by merchants and often read in secret,

---

[27] https://en.wikipedia.org/wiki/Robert_Louis_Stevenson, accessed March 22, 2017.

Knox encouraged the spread of home Bible study fellowships. People other than clergy seldom had copies of the Bible to read.

His fiery sermons often contradicted the views of Queen Mary Stuart. Allegedly she had him arrested and tried for treason in 1560 but he was acquitted. She is reported to have said, "I fear the prayers of John Knox more than all the armies of England."[28] By the time Knox died the Scottish Parliament had adopted the Reformation.

The more we toured other places in Scotland, the more I loved it. Listening to a special song on the tour bus about Scotland, "These are my mountains and I have come home." I truly felt at home as my sister and I toured where my mother's forefathers/ancestors from the clan Lamont lived before coming to America.[29]

I was glad to see places in Edinburgh where Eric Liddell spent time, including the university because he is one of my historical heroes. During the 1924 Olympics he refused to race on Sunday. But that week he went on to win a gold medal in the 400-meter race. After more schooling, he went to China as a missionary. He died in a Japanese prison camp during World War II after mentoring many young people while they were all prisoners. (See the movie "Chariots of Fire" about his Olympics challenge.)

Prayer: Thank You, Father for opportunities to take a glimpse back in time and get a better picture of what some of those we have long admired really went through to achieve their goals and dreams. Many of us have been indirectly affected when we ponder about their great contribution to literature, religion, and culture. Amen.

Scripture: "By no means do I count myself an expert in all of this, but I've got my eye on the goal, where God is beckoning us

---

[28] Carl Townsend, *Begin The Adventure*, (August 1, 2011) Creatingnewworlds.org.what-did-the-queen-of-Scotland-fear. Accessed March 22, 2017.
[29] Quin Sherrer, *Cast Your Shadow: Influence on Purpose*. (Kindle, 2018), 172-175.

onward—to Jesus. I'm off and running, and I'm not turning back." (Philippians 3:14b MSG)

Quin, a Star-Advocate newspaper feature writer, interviewed Apollo 13 astronaut Fred Haise at Titusville, Florida's Ti-Co Airport in summer of 1970 after his safe return following an aborted moon mission.

A Forty-Five Year Reunion

On January 23, 2015, I had the great opportunity to speak with Apollo 13 astronaut Fred Haise and give him a copy of a newspaper article I had written of my interview with him 45 years earlier. The article also had a photo of the two of us talking—I had my press camera in my hands.

PONDERING MY JOURNEY

My husband, a NASA engineer, had been in the control room on April 11, 1970, the day Fred Haise, Jack Swigert, and James A. Lovell, the mission commander, were launched into space headed for a moon landing. I observed the liftoff from outdoor bleachers reserved for the press while covering the launch for the Titusville Star Advocate newspaper.

However, Apollo 13 never completed its intended moon mission. An oxygen tank on board exploded, leaving the crew without electricity and water—200,000 miles from earth. When smoke filled the cabin following the explosion, the astronauts were in extreme danger. They used their lunar module as a lifeboat of sorts for the duration of the mission, though it was designed to sustain just two astronauts on the surface of the moon for a day and a half. They powered down to the lowest levels possible in order to conserve power.

During their four-day crisis, the astronauts endured with severely restricted water and food rations. And with limited power, the temperature was extremely cold.

President Richard Nixon asked the nation to pray for their safe return. Our family attended one of those prayer meetings held in our county during those suspenseful days. At the Space Center in Houston engineers, astronauts, and NASA personnel worked around the clock, using their skills and expertise to save them. And they did. The astronauts splashed down in the Pacific Ocean near Samoa on April 17, 1970, thanks to the efforts of many—and God answering prayer.

Some weeks later those astronauts came back to Kennedy Space Center to thank the personnel involved in their launch. Sitting in the newspaper office that summer day, I had a sudden hunch that they would probably fly out of our local airport soon. Turning to Nancy, a reporter sitting beside me, I said, "Grab a camera and let's go find an astronaut." I told my editor where we were headed. He waved us off with his "okay."

Sure enough when we drove up, I spotted all three waiting to board their plane but I chose to speak with Fred Haise while they waited. After showing him my press badge, I began to interview him. Nancy snapped our picture while I took notes. My article was published soon afterwards in one of the larger newspaper affiliates.

Forty-five years later my opportunity to speak with Haise again came backstage after he was keynote speaker at a Chautauqua Assembly event in DeFuniak Springs, Florida—a town where my parents lived before my birth and where I was married. In fact, one of my daughters had taught in the very high school where he spoke to the Chautauqua audience.

As he lectured, Haise showed a video of a portion of their journey along with pictures of Kennedy Space Center. I recognized a few engineer friends in the control room photos.

As I heard Haise speak that morning in 2015 my mind flashed back to that summer day 45 years earlier when I felt prompted to go after that special interview. During our conversation now I told him about the many people in our Brevard County area who attended prayer watches held for him and his space travelers during their uncertain future. He had listened closely.[30]

A great memory for me and a great short "reunion"—brought back lots of happy-time memories of the various space launches I covered during my writing years with the Titusville newspaper. God honors memories—and can connect people even decades later. His timing is aways on time.

Prayer: Lord, thank You for special encounters and for happy memories—all made possible because You, Creator of heaven and earth, orchestrate our events. Thank You for experiences that leave

---

[30] Quin Sherrer, *Cast Your Shadow: Influence on Purpose*. (Kindle, 2018), 167-170.

a shadow on us even years later. I was blessed. I am blessed. Amen.

Scripture: "We live within the shadow of the Almighty, sheltered by the God who is above all gods. This I declare, that he alone is my refuge, my place of safety; he is my God, and I am trusting him." (Psalm 91:1 TLB)

Part Ten: Lessons from Those Who Lived Before Us

A Mother Enters Heaven

My mother, a brave 72-year-old who had single-handedly raised four youngsters, was nearing the end of her fight against cancer. She and I both knew her time on earth was short.

She told her oncologist, "My hope is not in chemotherapy or radiation—it is in the Lord. Whether I live or I die, I'm the Lord's."

She had submitted to those treatments with their horrible side effects, even losing all her hair. Then another hospital stay. But when the time in this hospital was running out, the doctor said she could go home or to a rehab facility. She wanted to die in her home, and I wanted to honor her request. My husband and I had already moved into her house in Destin, Florida to help care for her for the past year.

I sought the advice of the hospital social services worker about taking her home. As she shared a list of nurse's aides who did homecare into my hand, her words to me were something I could never forget.

"I'm sure your mom will say or do something so special you will always remember and cherish the moment. In fact, you will be glad you took her home regardless of the hardship it may be to care for her and see her suffer."

So, we hired two aides—one for night shift and another for the day to help me give her meds, turn her, change her, bathe her, and keep her comfortable as she was completely bedridden. But there were several hours early in the morning between their shifts. My sister Ann flew in help from time to time too.

Mom had slipped into a "semi-comatose state," not speaking or opening her eyes. But on that early morning her blue eyes popped open after the aide left at five. Her eyes stared straight ahead. I waved my hand in front of her face. No response. I leaned over to kiss her and talk to her as though she could understand everything.

"Today is my fiftieth birthday, Mom. Remember when I was born at Grandma Beatrice's home? I am going to say the Lord's Prayer. You just agree with me." I prayed "Our Father" aloud, then repeated Psalm 23 as I always did each morning before cranking her hospital bed higher to reposition her.

Flipping on a tape recording of her favorite choruses and hymns, I then left for the kitchen to get a cup of coffee. Soon I heard a stirring and ran to Mom's bedroom. The recording was playing "Open my eyes, Lord. I want to see Jesus." But it was Mom who had made the sound.

Ann and I watched as through clenched teeth Mom gave a weak shout, "Hallelujah! Hallelujah! Hallelujah!" Three times. That was all. A faint smile played across her face. Still, she showed no recognition of us. Had she heard me talking with her earlier? Had she seen a glimpse of heaven? Seen Jesus?

Then I remembered the hospital social worker telling me, "I'm sure your mom will say or do something so special you will always cherish it." What a birthday gift to me.

She never uttered another word and a few days later, one afternoon three days after Easter, she took her last breath in her own bedroom. Ann and I prayed over her. When her pastor arrived 20 minutes later, we prayed with him as we committed her to the Lord.

I could rejoice. A year and four weeks of fighting this battle was over. The victory was won. A saint—my Mama Jewett—had entered heaven.

When I told close friends the exact time mother had died, I learned some had at that very moment heard God's gentle voice to pray for her—escorting her in prayer into the heavenlies to meet face to face with Jesus whom she loved so passionately.

Fran and Effie, Mom's two prayer partners, gathered in a home to pray specifically for her as she was breathing her last. Carol stopped her housework and went to walk on the beach beside her house to intercede for her. Laura, 450 miles away in Melbourne, Florida, put down the manuscript she was working on and walked out on her screen porch to pray for her. Aunt Betty in California—clear across the States—picked up her Bible and said a special prayer for Mom.

All this went on as Mom was entering heaven. Oh, the blessedness of intercessors. How comforting to learn God had spoken to each of these women friends in a quiet way and prompted them to stop and pray for Mother.[31]

Moments to cherish. A social worker and friends to thank. Mom to honor. God to praise! Why not tell someone about your special never-to-be-forgotten event. I'm sure you have one.

Prayer: Almighty Father, I am so grateful for my mother. And for the assurance that she is now in heaven. Thankful too for her steadfast love for You which she passed on to many others. Thank

---

[31] Quin Sherrer, *Good Night, Lord*. (Ventura, CA: Regal Books, 2002), 84-86.

You also for friends who hear Your voice to intercede at the exact minute they are needed. Bless them and help me keep alert to pray for them when I am needed. In Jesus' name I ask. Amen.

Scriptures: "She watches over the ways of her household and does not eat the bread of idleness. Her children rise up and call her blessed." (Proverbs 31: 27, 28a NKJV)

"Hear my prayer, O LORD, And give ear to my cry; Do not be silent at my tears; For I am a stranger with You, A sojourner, as all my fathers were." (Psalm 39:12 NKJV)

My Widow's Lesson

During stormy times in our life, it is comforting to seek the Lord for direction and hope. For me it happened one winter afternoon in a cemetery—after I had recently become a widow.

I spread a green blanket beside my husband's grave and plopped down. Opening my small Bible, I began to read it aloud, asking the Lord to again reassure me of His promises for my future. My husband had graduated to heaven recently and Christmas, just days away, would mark our 54th wedding anniversary.

I began with Psalm 23, "The Lord is my Shepherd, I shall not want." Personalizing Psalm 121, I yelled into the wind, "The Lord is my Keeper. The Lord will protect me from all evil; He will keep my soul; He will guard my going out and my coming in forever." Six times, that psalm repeats keeps, or preserves, meaning God is my caregiver. "The Lord is my Provider. He will meet all my needs, according to His riches in glory…. The Lord is my Comforter…"

For the next 30 minutes, I decreed comforting psalms, warfare Scriptures, prophetic verses—all the while letting God's precious Word minister to my heart.

The Lord seemed to whisper to me, "What do you see?" Looking around, I observed many gravesites and realized I was alone in the cemetery. Before I could respond to His question, His voice came again. "Everyone here is dead. You are the only one alive. So, get up and act alive!" Yes, that is what I had come to hear. My turning-around point. I would go home and celebrate Christ's birthday and my anniversary.

Placing a flag on LeRoy's military marker in Destin cemetery. Quin's mother is buried nearby.

That afternoon I declared: "The Lord's keeping power will sustain me. I am alive, and He will guide me on this difficult new journey."[32]

What about you? Do you have a desperate need? Why not let our heavenly Father minister to you through His Word? He has many hope-filled promises in it for you too!

Prayer: Lord, thank You that You never leave us nor forsake us. Amen.

---

[32] Quin Sherrer, *Hope for a Widow's Heart*. (Franklin, TN: Authentic Publishers, 2013), 3-5.

Scriptures: "Now may the God of hope fill you with all joy and peace in believing, that you many abound in hope by the power of the Holy Spirit." (Romans 15:13 NKJV)

"The Lord will watch over your coming and going both now and forevermore." (Psalm 121:8)

Burying Loved Ones During Pandemic

"People deserve a right to be remembered and their life celebrated, but we've been robbed even of the opportunity to honor the dead," a friend told me during the pandemic. We were not allowed to assemble to pay our last respects to those we loved—family or friends who had impacted our lives so deeply.

My brother, James, a well-loved attorney, died on a Sunday. He was buried Thursday in a private graveside service attended by his wife, their children and spouses, one grandchild, and a preacher. No church service. No friends to say goodbye. The small service was an effort to prevent others from being exposed to Covid-19. New normal? I hoped not.

Three weeks before my brother's death, my precious Anglican pastor, Forrest Mobley, died of heart failure while clutching his comfort cross. A few days earlier he called me, "I will be meeting Jesus soon, but I wanted to tell you I love you," he whispered. We both cried. He was my friend and often a spiritual advisor for more than four decades. There was no funeral. Someday there will be a memorial service for him.

Then there was my first cousin, Sue, buried with only a limited family gathering because of their state's strict "no crowds" regulations. As they were properly distanced around her grave, three of them sang "Amazing Grace." (One sibling was absent, having tested positive for the virus the day before.)

Though I was unable to go to my brother's graveside service, I flipped through old pictures—remembering, laughing, crying. Photos of him growing up in our mother's boarding house, high school graduation, earning his law degree, his wedding, birth of his four children, years volunteering with the Boy Scouts and even hiking with them after he turned 80. Serving as city attorney, city judge, receiving awards. Wearing his top hat to give historical lectures to civic groups and posing with the books he wrote about our county. Not long afterwards, his wife died.

And then some weeks later while still under lockdown status in most states, my only sister's husband died. Only their small family attended his short graveside service.

What happened to our society during this pandemic?[33] While my relatives who died did not have the virus, most of us knew someone who did. While stringent state restrictions keep many people house-bound, public health authorities said they were needed.

I began writing a few more thank-you letters and making a few more phone calls to give accolades to folks I cherish so they will know how much they have meant to me—while we are all still alive, fulfilling our destiny on earth. Perhaps you too will want to make some contacts with those you treasure.

Prayer: Father, I am thankful that Jesus Christ suffered and died for our sins. And that He rose again, was seen by hundreds, and then ascended to heaven. He has prepared a place for His followers to join Him someday. I'm also glad believers can look forward to reunions in heaven. Father, I thank You for all the wonderful people who have enriched my life. Help me find ways to honor them. Amen.

Scripture: "Truly, truly, I [Jesus] say to you, he who hears My word, and believes Him who sent Me, has eternal life, and does not come into judgment, but has passed out of death into life." (John 5:24 NKJV)

---

[33] Covid-19 pandemic (Dec. 2019-2022—depending on various regulations).

Roots and Heritage from Grandparents

"Build on your roots and heritage," the big sign read. I pondered that thought for quite a while. Roots and heritage. The words tumbled over and over in my mind, though I was not sure what they meant to me. Maybe parents and grandparents?

I don't remember a grandmother who blessed or prayed for me—which is what I would want as a portion of my heritage.

"A blessing is a word spoken for good that carries spiritual power and authority, and that sets in motion something that will probably go on from generation to generation," writes my pastor friend Dr. James W. Goll.[34]

My maternal grandmother died soon after I, the first granddaughter, was born in her home. Her last words were, "Has the baby had her milk?" She was thinking of me! My paternal grandmother was a pastor's wife, and we kids loved going to her home, but I never knew if she prayed for her 14 grandchildren. Or blessed us with her words.

I do remember as a preteen sitting on a stool at the feet of my blind great-grandmother Josie—my mother's grandmother—whose brothers had fought in the Civil War. She rested her hand on the top of my head, felt my face. Did she bless or pray for me? I'd want to think so, but I will never know.

A few weeks after I saw that "Roots and Heritage" sign, I'd finished speaking at a retreat in Mississippi near where my daddy was buried. My friend Freda offered to drive me an hour south so I could visit his grave. When they had his funeral, I was speaking at a Christian seminar in another country.

Now we drove down asphalt backroads, passing fields dotted with blooming magnolia and dogwood trees. Finally, we saw a

---
[34] James W. Goll, "Invoking the Power of the Blessing," *Elijah List*, accessed, Nov. 29, 2015.

sign pointing to Sharon Cemetery, established in 1827. We drove around until I spotted his tombstone. Getting out of the car, I walked about, trying to sort through my mixed emotions. Daddy had abandoned mother with four children when I, the oldest, was barely a teen. He had married the other woman in his life and never got close to his children after that.

One summer night, when I was 30-something, I chose to forgive my dad in a very emotional life-changing experience while kneeling in a pastor's office. I chose to forgive Dad based on what God's Word required of me. When he was advanced in age, he made two short visits to see me in our home—travelling alone by bus. And I truly did feel a love for him. One night he asked me, "How could you forgive and love me after all I've done?"

Now as I stood over his grave, my eye was drawn also to the grave of my beloved granddad buried on the other side of his son—my dad.

Through the years, Granddaddy had given my mother encouragement when he stayed with us on occasional visits—even though she was his former daughter-in-law. Whenever he dropped in, he was also my cheerleader—my father figure. "Girl," he would say to me, "You can do anything you set your mind to do if God is in it. He'll equip and help you."

When this grandaddy, a Presbyterian minister, performed my wedding ceremony, he laid his hand on my head and pronounced a beautiful biblical blessing. He further blessed me by asking God's favor—for my happiness and other good things, but most of all for me to fulfill God's will and destiny.

He was 83 the last time he came to see me when we lived near Kennedy Space Center. I took him to watch Apollo 14 blast into space as we stood on the riverbank in our town. "Spectacular!" he shouted. Later at the Space Center Museum, I watched him gawk at the gray rock Neil Armstrong had brought back from the moon.

PONDERING MY JOURNEY

Trying to comprehend this moon-walk milestone, Grandaddy told me about his thrill at seeing his first automobile—a Model T-Ford—over 60 years earlier. "What progress we've made," he said, shaking his head in wonder as he studied the moon rock. Grandaddy went on to live into his 90s.[35]

At those gravesites that afternoon as other memories surfaced, I recognized that Grandaddy was an important part of my roots and heritage. I had never been abandoned. I bowed my head in the silence of that cemetery and thanked God for my forefathers and foremothers—my roots and heritage.

Today as a grandmother myself, I wonder what wonders my descendants will experience. I hope they will all know that this grandmother has planted plenty of prayers and spoken aloud many blessings for them—-building on my roots and heritage.

Have you considered how you might speak blessings over your family? Or plant prayers for the youngest generation following you?

Prayer: Thank You, Lord, for our parents, grandparents, and other ancestors who have gone before us—for the commendable capabilities and talents they passed on to their next generations. Help us to so live that we will leave inspiring spiritual footprints for ours to follow. In the name of Jesus, I pray. Amen.

Scriptures: "I will pour My Spirit on your descendants, and My blessing on your offspring." (Isaiah 44:3 NKJV)

"The Lord bless you and keep you; The Lord make His face shine upon you, And be gracious to you; The Lord lift up His countenance upon you, And give you peace." (Numbers 6:24-26 NKJV)

---

[35] Quin Sherrer, *Good Night, Lord*. (Ventura, CA: Regal Books, 2000), 175.

Joining Generations in a Cemetery

When we stroll through old country cemeteries searching for specific graves where our forefathers and foremothers are buried, some of us may be seeking more information on our family roots—our heritage.

"Heritage is a person's unique, inherited sense of family identity: the values, traditions, culture, and artifacts handed down by previous generations."[36]

Grave markers can provide insight into the history of our families and can help us commemorate the life of those who have gone before us.

I believe we need to remember and honor our loved ones who have lived before us. On a recent fall day, I had a memorable adventure and did just that. I had come from another state hoping my daughter could help me locate the burial place of my maternal grandmother in Southern Alabama. After driving a while, we finally located the cemetery which opened in 1856.

I sat in the car letting my eyes roam over the many old gravestones as my daughter walked about, winding her way among the oldest graves. She searched for a full hour as the hot sun beat down on her.

Finally, she found it—a brown-colored grave marker the exact size of a coffin, lying flat on the ground, with the inscription at the head showing Grandmother Beatrice's name, and dates of her birth and death. My daughter waved for me to come see what she had discovered, so I walked through the uneven sandy ground to stand beside her.

I had never seen a gravestone the shape and color of my grandmother's—there was no mold or lichen on it. Just unusual brown in color and shape.

---

[36] www:familysearch.org in blog "What is Heritage?"

PONDERING MY JOURNEY

But then came the biggest surprise! Beside the grave of Grandmother Beatrice were the graves of her mother, my great-grandmother Josephene born in 1863, and my great-great grandmother Malisia, born in 1814, who was Josephene's mother-in-law. Malisia's cement stone had crumbled into three pieces, but I could read the information on it.

We had found three grandmothers when I had only been hoping to find one! Yet, I knew a bit about two of these grandmas' Christian beliefs and how they "fit" into our family line.

But I was not familiar with a Sarah born in 1832 or still another born in 1812 with our family's last name who were buried near the others. Discovering facts about these women will require some online searches.

As I stood at Beatrice's site—Mother's mom's grave—the grandmother I'd never known because she died shortly after I was born, I began to picture what it must have been like for my mother and dad to stand here on this very spot together almost 90 years ago. And watch the body of mom's 52-year-old mother lowered into the ground while Mother cuddled me, their firstborn, in her arms.

I continued to wonder about my mother's emotions. I had been told she had come from Florida to Alabama to assist her dying mother who lived alone. I was born in her house three months later. Dr. Doughty, who had delivered Mom, delivered me, and did not charge for his call. Mother must have been lonely because my dad was off in graduate school three states away and could not come for my birth. But because Grandmother Beatrice died in summer, he got there for her burial in a town some miles from her home. My parents were surely comforted to know she had gone to heaven to be with her Savior.

Grandmother had worked for a telephone company, keeping the switchboard in her house, and was known as "Central" to her customers. My mother, who had been a telephone supervisor before her marriage, continued to operate the switchboard while her mom was so sick.

Beatrice's own mother, Josephene ("Josie") outlived her by 16 years. For many years she managed a large farm, but she also taught Bible lessons to children and adults. I had the opportunity to visit her once before she died at 86. By then she was blind, but I sat at her feet while she told me stories of her childhood. The baby of 12 children, she got married at 15 and was a grandmother by age 36. Her family buried her beside her oldest daughter.

Inscribed on Josephene's headstone are two hands clasped and both have matching sleeve cuffs. "When the two clasped hands have the same cuff at the same level it can mean farewell, goodbye to earthly life and a greeting to eternal life," according to an Internet explanation.

I said a silent prayer at each gravesite, thanking God for these women—my foremothers.

As we drove away from the country cemetery, I remembered that sign I had seen some years ago. "Build on your roots and heritage." Here in this unfamiliar place—a graveyard no less—I had indeed again discovered some more of my roots and heritage. And enjoyed an awesome day too!

When I got back home, I read again the yellowed notes and letters written some years ago about these two grandmothers by an aunt who knew them well. As I did, I was grateful for their Christian heritage which they lived out. I was blessed.

But I also recognized that when we read through family history, we may find that some of our deceased relatives made wrong choices and mistakes—just like we do. Yet we absorb a sense of our heritage throughout our lives as we observe and experience the things that make our family unique.

Have you, dear reader, considered your roots and heritage too? Have you considered thanking the Lord for your ancestors?

PONDERING MY JOURNEY

If you did not know your deceased relatives, visiting their gravesites may help you learn interesting facts you never knew, especially if they have epitaphs, or short sayings, carved on them. Many modern gravestones include biographical details, photographs, and even quotes or poems.

What about the graves of relatives we may never visit? Like those who served in the military. Over the years I've listened to uncles, cousins, and even my youngest brother relate personal experiences. During World War II, my mother's cousin Hughy barely survived the long Bataan Death March in the Philippines during the spring of 1945. Prisoners of war were forced by the Japanese to walk to their eventual prison camp. Thousands died during the march and imprisonment. In his latter years, Hughy told me that when he was an Alabama farm boy, he had learned how to chew sugar cane. So, as a POW he searched at night until he found cane along the death march. But he stressed that he had a strong will to live, while asking God for strength to survive. Personal accounts like these have touched my heart with gratitude for those who serve our country.

One of my writing teachers, Arthur Gordon, writes in his book *Return to Wonder*:

> The way we live now, ancestors tend to fade very quickly, we hardly know them at all. But now and then one will step out of the shadows to remind us that they did precede us, that they were real people of flesh and blood, and that in a deep invisible sense they are still living in us.[37]

Prayer: Thank You, Lord, for our parents, grandparents, and other ancestors who have gone before us—for the commendable capabilities and talents they passed on to their next generations.

---

[37] Arthur Gordon, *Return to Wonder*. (Nashville, TN: Broadman & Holman Publishers, 1996), 127.

Help us to so live that we will leave inspiring spiritual footprints for ours to follow. In the name of Jesus, I pray. Amen.

Scriptures: "Which He commanded our fathers, that they were to teach them to their children, So that the generation to come would know, the children yet to be born, that they would arise and tell them to their children. So that they would put their confidence in God. And not forget the works of God but comply with His commandments." (Psalm 78:5b-7 NASB)

"I will pour My Spirit on your descendants, and My blessing on your offspring." (Isaiah 44:3 NKJV)

"Yes, even when I am old and gray-headed, O God, forsake me not, [but keep me alive] until I have declared Your mighty strength to [this] generation, and Your might and power to all that are to come." (Psalm 71:18 AMPC)

My Forefather Was a Christian

Duncan Lammon (Lamont), one of my "forefathers" on my mom's side of the family, arrived in America in 1775 from Scotland. His ship landed in Cape Fear, North Carolina, as best I can determine.

On November 4, 1798, he wrote his will. I was glad to find this because it told me that this one of my forefathers was a Christian, very much dedicated to the Lord. And he wanted to be sure his family was cared for after his death!

His last will and testament reads:

"In the name of God, 'Amen' I, Duncan Lamont, Planter in Bladen county and state of North Carolina, through the mercy of God, yet though weak in body yet of perfect understanding and memory, blessed be God, do constitute to this my last will and testament:

"I humbly bequeath my soul to Almighty God, my maker, beseeching his most gracious acceptance of it through the merit and meditations of my most compassionate Redeemer, Jesus Christ.

PONDERING MY JOURNEY

"I order that my lawful debts be paid in the first place. I order my house and half of my plantation and half of the woods land to my beloved wife during her lifetime and then to return to my son Duncan and heirs, half; and to Daniel half. I leave to my beloved wife furniture, bed, chest. I order one cow for my eldest daughter Marian. I order one cow and calf for my eldest son. I order one-half of a two-year old mare for my two youngest daughters…"

This will sound strange in 21st century America. While I don't know much more about this early relative who settled in America, I am glad to have this proof of his faith in Jesus Christ.

Prayer: Lord, thank You for our brave relatives who made the voyage to America to live. I especially thank You for the Christian heritage they brought and left for the next generations to follow. Help us be faithful to pass the torch of Christianity to the generations that follow us. I ask in the name of Jesus. Amen.

Scripture: "And the Lord had said to Abram, 'Get out of your country, from your family and from your father's house, to the land I will show you…I will bless you…And you shall be a blessing.'" (Genesis 12:1-2 NKJV)

Part Eleven: Living Your Dash Well

Finishing Your Race

Most gravestones have a dash between the birthday and the death of the person buried there. Linda Ellis wrote a famous poem called "The Dash" challenging us to live our lives well between the dash—from our birth to our death. She asks when our eulogy is being read with our "life's actions to rehash," would we be proud of how we spent our dash?[38]

Newspaper obituaries often tell life stories in glowing terms, listing the deceased's many accomplishments. Occasionally you read a candid straightforward obituary. Let me share those about two friends of mine. I hope they will cause you to smile—as I do whenever I reread them.

When our friend Billy, a pharmacist for 39 years, died after a 13-year battle with cancer, his children wrote his obituary. It started out: "Billy loved vanilla ice cream. He was real and he loved real people. He could spot a phony a mile away. He was disarmingly truthful…He loved God and his church family…We his family do not mourn his passing because we are in full knowledge that Billy is with his beloved Father in heaven."

---

[38] Linda Ellis, www:lindaellis.net/the dash

PONDERING MY JOURNEY

After other details, the obit ended: "In lieu of flowers, please send fried chicken." And folks who came to honor him at his funeral did enjoy fried chicken afterwards in a home while swapping funny stories about him.

This comical idea of sharing fried chicken instead of flowers made the rounds among our close friends. We'd laugh about fried chicken being the preferred entrée when we Southerners gathered for a comfort meal or a pot-luck dinner.

The next year on an August Sunday afternoon my husband died. My daughters and I stayed a while afterwards at the hospice facility located in a different town from where we lived. Lingering to pray and say our goodbyes, we also called a few close friends to let them know.

We had not been home long when my doorbell rang. Standing at my front door was Brett, the adult son of one of our friends we had called. He handed me a big bucket of Colonel Sanders Kentucky fried chicken. He didn't have to explain why—his mom had already shared with him how much we liked chicken, and they knew we had a house full of relatives to feed. Thanking Brett, I even smiled a moment, remembering Billy's obituary.

Then there was Deloris who lived in a little town not far from me. It had one traffic light, one grocery store, and one real estate office—hers. Whenever several friends stopped by her office at the same time for coffee, we had a powerful prayer meeting. After her husband and one son died, her other son came to help her. He wrote her obituary which expressed her life boldly.

"On a glorious blue-sky afternoon on April 16, the Heavens in indescribable majesty welcomed Deloris..." After listing her business achievements, it ended with this:

"The Lord blessed Deloris with His heart. She was quick to give if you were in need. Should you whisper to her "pray for me" in Kelly's [grocery store], be prepared for an out loud, Pentecostal, hell-shaking, hallelujah response right there between the Jim

Dandy grits and the black-eyed peas. The world has lost another warrior of righteousness and Heaven has received another faithful servant. She will be sorely missed."[39]

"I have fought the good fight, I have finished the race, I have kept the faith," Paul wrote his spiritual son, Timothy. Isn't that a wonderful challenge for us as well? To finish our sojourn on earth by keeping our faith in Christ?

The promise completing that Scripture verse is wonderful. "Now there is in store for me the crown of righteousness, which the Lord, the righteous Judge will award to me on that day—and not only to me, but also to all who have longed for his appearing." (2 Timothy 4:7-8)

So, what is the take-away of our life? What will others remember? What will our obituary say? More important, what will our Maker say?

Our race is still being run. When our earthly journey ends, don't we want it said that we finished the race well? Isn't that your desire?

Prayer: Lord, thank You for sustaining us from our birth to our eventual passing—all those in-between years we have been privileged to live. Help us run our race well. Thank You for the crown of righteousness that awaits us when we meet You. Help us leave footprints of faith for our descendants to follow. We pray in the name of Jesus, our Savior. Amen.

Scriptures: "I am God, and there is none like Me, Declaring the end from the beginning." (Isaiah 46:9b,10a NKJV)

"And let us run with endurance the race that is set before us, looking unto Jesus, the author and finisher of our faith, who for the joy that was set before Him endured the cross, despising

---

[39] Deloris Merritt, Obituary, *Northwest Florida Daily News*, Ft. Walton Beach, FL: April 19, 2008.

PONDERING MY JOURNEY

the shame, and has sat down at the right hand of the throne of God." (Hebrews 12:1b-2 NKJV)

"I have fought the good (worthy, honorable, and noble) fight, I have finished the race, I have kept (firmly held) the faith." (2 Timothy 4:7 AMPC)

Turning 90 in March 2023, Quin was joined by friends Tes, Beth, JoNell, Kerry, and Ceci who celebrated with her in Destin, Florida. She laughs when they put a tiara on her head.

Jesus in the Operating Room

August 2023

Jesus in the operating room? The picture on the wall in the waiting room of the surgeon's office gave me courage. While waiting to consult with this specialist I had never met, the painting told me all I needed to know about the man I would trust to operate on me—to implant a pacemaker.

The picture shows three figures in an operating room all dressed in sterile blue gowns and gloves. Instruments are laid out and obviously surgery is underway. The lead surgeon's hand is up. Standing right behind him is the figure of Jesus, touching his hand, as though guiding him as he performs the operation.[40]

Yes, I had chosen the right doctor. The unspoken message came when I studied this painting. Jesus would be the unseen Physician in the operating room with my doctor and all of those involved in my procedure.

"Look," I said excitedly to others sitting in the waiting room. Pointing toward the picture, I continued, "Look, folks at that picture. Jesus will be in the operating room when this doctor operates on us." One man walked over to view the picture more closely. After a while, he smiled and said, "Glad the Great Physician will be there. It's reassuring."

When I finally met the doctor, I thanked him for that inspiring work of art and explained how it encouraged me. You see I had faced fear that at my age—90 years—being put to sleep again and cut open was risky. It was a fear I was overcoming. How glad I was to meet a fellow believer who counts on Christ for wisdom and guidance. His Christian focus is clear to anyone who enters his office.

A few days later in the hospital as I was being prepared for surgery, the anesthesiologist came to talk to me first. I told her that I had prayed for whoever would administer anesthesia for me. But I also told her about the picture in the doctor's office. "Jesus will be in the operating room with us—you and all those working on

---

[40] To view the painting on the web, look for "Chief of the Medical Staff" by artist Nathan Greene, or the link "Paintings of Jesus in Operating Room." Website details read: "Greene's gift for detail rendered in luminous color shines in this powerful image. Patients and their loved ones can find strength in its reminder that we are always in God's care, even when we are most vulnerable."

me." She smiled and said she understood as she had attended parochial school.

I even told a few other medical personnel in the O.R.—Jesus would be there with us. It didn't matter whether they believed me or not. I knew Jesus promised that He would never leave nor forsake me. I was put to sleep, the surgery performed, and I was rolled into a hospital bed to begin recovery. I had no problem waking up!

The next day this surgeon stood beside my hospital bed, grasped my hand, and we prayed. A moving, encouraging moment for me!

Prayer: Lord, Thank You for Christians in the medical field who help us. And thank You that Jesus never leaves us. Amen.

Scripture: "And Jesus having heard, said to them, 'They who are whole have no need of a physician, but they who are ill'" (Matthew 9:12 YLT).

A Surprise Diagnosis

While God planned the beginning of our lives, only He knows the ending. Yet we have had the privilege of doing the living!

While I face another challenging health issue, I know Jesus is with me. And He always will be until I finish my race on earth. Then He will welcome me to heaven.

I received a surprise diagnosis two months after my 90th birthday bash when I was admitted to the hospital while coughing up blood. I had inoperable lung cancer. I am still puzzled over that diagnosis because I never smoked and was not around others who did. As mentioned earlier, following surgery and radiation for breast cancer, I was pronounced cancer-free.

Lung cancer and fluid on the lungs. I went home from the hospital eight days later with a list of doctors to see soon. But first I needed a heart surgeon to implant a pacemaker to keep my pulse from going too low from AFib. So that surgery was first.

Friends and family drove me to my 33 radiation treatments which left me exhausted. But I tried to finish this book when I rested up.

Age 90. Christmas 2023 in Niceville, Florida.

Now as I write this, very close to my 91st birthday, I am awaiting more tests and various doctors' recommendations. "You are not out of the woods yet," the oncologist cautioned me.

I am most grateful to those many friends, relatives, and pastors who are praying for me and for their texts, calls, and cards. I am thankful too for each medical caregiver I've had—every doctor, nurse, physical therapist, and technician!

Most of all I am grateful for Jesus who can readily identify with our suffering and pain. While hanging on the cross, He endured a terrible crucifixion, willingly dying for our sins. Scripture says He is "touched with the feeling of our infirmities" (Hebrews 4:15 KJV).

Whether our illness is short-lived or ongoing, He meets us with great compassion. He healed people by different means under various conditions during His three years of earthly ministry.

I am always open for His supernatural touch, His complete healing! I welcome it. Yet, I am truly grateful for modern medical advances and for my various Christian doctors who also believe that the Lord Jesus is with us through our ill health ordeals. And they use their skills to help us.

Prayer: Lord, I do need Your healing power. Thank You for being with me and my doctors and other medical personnel during my recent hospitalizations and treatments. Thank You for continuing to be with my doctors and technicians in whatever lies ahead in the way of treatments. Give them wisdom. Thank You, my loving Savior, Jesus Christ, who will always be with me. Amen.

Scriptures: "But those who wait for Yahweh's grace will experience divine strength. They will rise up on soaring wings and fly like eagles, run their race without growing weary, and walk through life without giving up." (Isaiah 40:31 TPT)

"He was wounded for our transgressions; He was bruised for our iniquities." (Isaiah 53:5a NKJV)

"The Lord himself goes before you and will be with you; he will never leave you nor forsake you. Do not be afraid; do not be discouraged." (Deuteronomy 31:8)

The Future

One thing is sure: God holds my future.

I am extremely grateful for my warrior friends praying for my complete recovery. I rest in Jesus' destiny for me—regardless of His timing for my homegoing to heaven.

One Scripture God spoke to Joshua is precious to me: "Have I not commanded you? Be strong and of good courage; do not be afraid nor be dismayed, for the Lord your God is with you wherever you go." (Joshua 1:9 NKJV)

"Those who love God never meet for the last time!" said Eric Liddell (1902-1945).

And so do I have that assurance—with family and a multitude of friends.

As I finish pondering my journey I want to end with this Scripture:

"The promise of 'arrival' and 'rest' is still there for God's people. God himself is at rest. And at the end of the journey, we'll surely rest with God. So let's keep at it and eventually arrive at the place of rest, not drop out through some sort of disobedience." (Hebrews 4:9-11 MSG)

Invite Jesus into Your Life

If you do not know Jesus as your Savior and Lord, here is a prayer you can pray:

Lord Jesus, please reveal Yourself to me. I want to know You in a real and personal way. I admit I am a sinner. Please forgive me for walking in my own selfish ways. I believe You are the Son of God who came to earth, died on the cross, and shed Your blood for my sins. I believe You rose from the dead and are seated at the right hand of the Father in heaven. I thank You for forgiving me of my sins. I receive You as my Lord and Savior. I want to live my life to please You. Please send the Holy Spirit to strengthen and empower me. Thank You for the free gift of salvation that will enable me to live with You forever. Amen.[41]

---

[41] Quin Sherrer, *Hope for a Widow's Heart*. (Franklin, TN: Authentic Publishers, 2013), 228.

Old Age

In old age, your body no longer serves you so well.
Muscles slacken, grip weakens, joints stiffen.
The shades are pulled down on the world.
You can't come and go at will. Things grind to a halt.
The hum of the household fades away.
You are wakened now by bird-song.
Hikes to the mountains are a thing of the past.
Even a stroll down the road has its terrors.
Your hair turns apple-blossom white,
Adorning a fragile and impotent matchstick body.
Yes, you're well on your way to eternal rest,
While your friends make plans for your funeral.

Life, lovely while it lasts, is soon over.
Life as we know it, precious and beautiful, ends.
The body is put back in the same ground it came from.
The spirit returns to God, who first breathed it.

(Ecclesiastes 12:4-7 MSG)

Copyright © 1993, 2002, 2018 by Eugene H. Peterson

America Needs Our Savior

Here is a prayer from our book *Warfare Prayers for Women*:

Prayer: Father, I pray for the enemy's assignments that are aligned against Your purposes for this nation to be demolished. Let those that are hidden be revealed and officials with malicious agendas be stopped and brought to justice. Lord, I pray for You to give all area and governmental leaders great wisdom concerning crucial decisions they will be making both in their public and private lives. Show them that being in a position of power to represent the well-being of their constituents is a sacred trust. Thank You that our Founders honored You by establishing our constitutional republic on prayer and the Scriptures. May that foundation be reinforced. Help us not to give in to fear and hopelessness but to stand steadfast on Your precious promises. I pray for a powerful spiritual awakening that will cause many people in this nation to receive Jesus' love and salvation. I ask in His name—the name above all names. Amen.[42]

---

[42] Quin Sherrer and Ruthanne Garlock, *Warfare Prayers for Women*. (Bloomington, MN: Chosen Books, 2020), 236, 244.

Part Twelve: Friends Pondering Their Journey with Quin

As Désirée and I finished the editing on this book, we decided that some of Quin's friends who have shared her journey might like the opportunity to write what her influence has been on them as they journeyed with her. So here are a few whom she has known for many years, pondering on their journey with her. *Sherry Anderson*

Désirée Schroeder—who edited this book for Quin—dressed in her wedding dress, with her mother, Sherry Anderson, at Désirée's wedding, a long-awaited answer to prayer.

PONDERING MY JOURNEY

Quin: My friend, my writing mentor, and the most diligent writer I know. In 1988, you took me to the Florida Christian Writers Conference, which was held at Peter Lord's church—my first. Then you invited me to drive us to writers' conferences in Houston and Orlando. I thank God for all the years I have known you. We shared a hotel room at an Aglow conference years ago. My stepdaughter, Rebecca, came with me. After sharing a room, you wrote about us in your next book—telling about our relationship and how my stepdaughter loved me back.

Your teaching as a keynote speaker at Aglow's International conference one year inspired me to be diligent in prayer for my "bean patch" made up of family members, spiritual leaders who influence me, and friends.

Then about writing—you are someone who always encouraged and challenged me to WRITE! Write articles! Write your story! Write, write, write. And who else could have done that for me, but someone disciplined to get up and write at 5:00 a.m. every morning. What an example. You've taught about your mentors and that made me think about who mentored me and who am I now influencing…I will pass it on. — ***Sherry Anderson***, *Florida Aglow State Leader, Author, Panama City, Florida*

Quin is such an inspiration in my life. She is a pen in our Lord's hand and obedient to write what He dictates. She genuinely loved my late husband, Forrest, who was her Anglican priest and friend. I will never be able to thank her enough for what that meant to him—and to me. —***Nancy Mobley***, *Saint Peter's Anglican Church, vestry member, Mountain Brook, Alabama*

When Quin and LeRoy lived in Colorado Springs (1993-2003), Dutch and I were honored to be their pastors. How do you pastor a prolific author, gifted speaker, and her iconic husband who had been an early NASA aerospace engineer? We always felt that they gave much more to us than we did them.

How do I describe Quin Sherrer and my relationship with her? She is always "on," ready to pray. If you don't know how to pray, she will teach you how! Quin is a remarkable speaker and skilled writer, which we all have benefited from. From time to time, we have used her posts in our *Give Him 15 Devotional* because they are so appropriate for our topic. Her relationship with Jesus is an inspiration, and she is a wonderful advisor. Not only is she willing to give advice when asked, but she will also take the need to our heavenly Father, being diligent and committed to pray.

All who know Quin personally, have her fingerprints on their lives. I am so very grateful to have known Quin for over 30 years (where did the time go), and her fingerprints are definitely on me. I thank Quin, for all she has given to me, as well as my family. I honor her and am so very grateful for her. — ***Ceci Sheets***, *Editor, Give Him 15 Devotional, Dutch Sheets Ministry, Batesburg-Leesville, South Carolina*

The impact of Quin's friendship, which started in 1993 in Colorado, has written something deep within my soul that I carry—a part of history retold, wisdom and insight of one who has pioneered being a woman of prayer and more importantly a woman of answered prayers.

I have a file with lots of teachings and stories Quin has shared with me. We've lived far apart for years now but we keep up weekly with each other by phone and email. I feel myself grabbing almost greedily for every word I can get. They are my treasures—words of wisdom, important history, opinions shared, insights, and stories of God in action.

PONDERING MY JOURNEY

In a dream I had recently, I saw Quin reaching her hand back to Corrie ten Boom, whom she had personally met. Then in this dream, while holding Corrie's hand, she reached for mine. I then reached out my hand to a younger group of people.

I do believe I am to "cast my shadow" on younger ones as she has done on me. Quin has placed not only her words but her heart into mine. She is a treasure to me, and I hope to give some of what she imparted to me to others. —**Beth Moore**, *Works for Dutch Sheets Ministry, Colorado Springs, Colorado*

I first heard of Quin Sherrer when I was training small group leaders in 1989 for Women's Aglow Fellowship in San Antonio and we were using one of her books. As a professional counselor at the time, I thought the book was excellent.

A few years later while visiting a friend in Colorado Springs I attended Dutch Sheets' church and was introduced to Quin Sherrer and Ruth Ann Garlock. My first thought was that these were powerful women to write all these Christian books. Before long I moved my counseling ministry to Colorado Springs. Quin and I spent lots of time together. If she had a speaking engagement high in the snow-covered mountains, I'd drive her because I had the right kind of car tires. And of course, I was her intercessor while she spoke.

Who knew Quin and I would walk a path together for over three decades—though we did not always live in the same city. Even in phone conversations today we have fun and laugh over the crazy things that happen in ministry. She adds a gift of humor to my life.

Quin works at being a great friend. There are times when I'm really on another wavelength but my friend listens and keeps confidences. This makes it easy to share my thoughts unhindered, feeling safe and protected.

As an intercessor, her prayer time for me has helped provide my protection as I've traveled near and far in my ministries— Mongolia, Ukraine, Germany, and ten summers in Africa. She fuels my desire to pray and persevere.

Quin challenges me with a phone call. "Have you written any of those stories yet?" She has hounded me about writing until I finally believe I have something to say and the capability to get it written. She has taught me so much and is like family to me even though we live 500 miles apart. —*Rev. Kerry Kathlene Bruton, President, Fountainhead Consulting, Deerfield Beach, Florida*

Back in 2002, when I was a student at the Wagner Leadership Institute in Colorado Springs, I had no clue I'd end up having such a lifelong treasured friendship with Quin, who was one of my favorite teachers there. I soon became the designated driver for Quin's speaking engagements. Those Colorado road trips were so much fun— delightful journeys!

Our husbands, LeRoy and Bruce, hit it off too, bonding over their shared love for aviation. So, we had tons of evenings filled with Mexican dinners and special holiday meals at our home. And you know what that means—more laughs! And more memories.

In 2004, I took on a church staff pastor role in the Dallas area, establishing a culture of prayer and intercession. No surprise, Quin became my biggest supporter and go-to advisor. She was the speaker for my first leadership retreat speaking on prayer and always— always—praying for each person that they would accomplish God's plans.

But Quin's wisdom didn't stop at prayer and leadership talks. Oh no, she generously mentored countless on the book-writing process. She coached us (yours truly included) through the maze of storytelling, research, and praying every step of the way. Three published books later, and she's still sure I have more books in me.

PONDERING MY JOURNEY

Looking back on all the laughs, deep conversations, and the prayer partnership we've built, I can't help but feel eternally grateful for being on this incredible journey with "Momma Quin." As she pondered her journey, I find myself in her shadow pondering mine. —*Mary Jo Pierce*, Author, Let It Rise, *Keller, Texas*

The Bible speaks often of the value of a faithful friend! When I met Quin, He gave me that and so much more. It is hard to wrap up in words just how priceless and precious her friendship has been to me, as are all things truly of eternal value. We first traveled together in 1992 to speak in Kansas at the Aglow area conference, and something in that time was forged deep in my soul. She is indeed one of a kind! She has been a friend first and with it came mentoring, encouragement, direction, grace, and so much love…and then add her prayers and I am a rich woman…the recipient of all of that and so much more.

We have shared adventures, hard times, tears, and lots of laughter. And with every conversation, no matter what is going on in her life I've heard, "Jo, let me pray for you." And off she goes!

We led a missions trip in Guatemala. It was an amazing time ministering to the people there. I watched as Quin blessed the children at the end of her message and, in truth, it opened up the whole church's heart to us. We roomed together and she taught me the value of a stainless-steel bowl she had brought with her! You could wash in it, shampoo your hair…you get the idea. Invaluable at the place where we stayed. We came back with so many stories and as we share them and reminisce, we laugh ourselves silly all over again.

I think I am Quin's laughter friend. Oh, I pray of course, and we share ministry…but she loves to laugh, and I seem to bring that medicine! She makes me laugh too…though she is most times very serious. We have called ourselves Lucy and Ethel. Sitting across from her in a Christian board meeting room you see her red lips flying—she's praying all the while.

How grateful I am for those prayers. She often says she has not gotten to go all the places I have though she has been to many countries. I have ministered in at least 25 nations, and I knew that Quin had her hands on her world map and was praying specifically for me and the people where I was ministering—especially on my many trips to Uganda and Kenya. That is a treasure beyond measure. I always look forward to bringing her back a report because she is certainly entitled to much of any reward!

I now have two books published—which she pushed me to write— and am working on a third, *Don't Waste Your Journey*. So, it is very appropriate for me to speak of the impact she's had on my journey. Whether by my side in prayer or presence, she's been a major contributor. She's a treasure the Lord placed squarely in my path, and I will forever be thankful. I love her dearly!

She's been my cheerleader and my champion, and I am more than blessed to have found a place in her heart! She is etched in mine. She's my Mama Quin! —*JoNell Gerland*, *President, Treasure In Clay International, Houston, Texas*

While attending a national conference in 1996 I heard Quin teach from her book *A House of Many Blessings*—the importance of taking care of our home and creating an environment that reflects our relationship with Christ. Several years later while serving as international president of Protestant Women of the Chapel, where we were both speakers at a regional PWOC conference, Quin urged me to keep sharing my testimony wherever I could. Today I'm an ordained minister, who continues to encourage military wives—whether their husbands are on active duty or retired. Not long ago Quin did a Zoom teaching from her home on her book

PONDERING MY JOURNEY

Cast Your Shadow: Influence on Purpose for 20 of our women scattered across the United States.

Quin's profound influence in my life and ministry has prepared me far beyond what I ever dreamed possible. She accurately spoke into my life and activated what I did not see. Before I knew her as a dear friend, I was changed by reading her book *A Woman's Guide to Spirit-Filled Living*. Hungry for more of God, I devoured its pages and found a prayer to pray for the baptism of the Holy Spirit which unlocked a deeper relationship with Christ than I ever thought possible. Her influence has helped me to courageously step out of my comfort zone to take on assignments and ministry roles I normally wouldn't have. I have been forever changed by her friendship, encouragement, and wise counsel. Both David and I have been blessed by her love and influence in our lives. Mama Quin has been a spiritual mother to me even across the many miles that separate us. —**Brenda Marlin**, *Former President, Protestant Women of the Chapel International, Florence, Texas*

My journey with Quin Sherrer started 33 years ago when I was a military wife, living in England and I purchased my first book by her, *How to Pray for Your Children*. Since then, I have lived in the same town as Quin and I have had the privilege to hear her speak at many events and have often accompanied her as a prayer partner. One of my greatest honors has been to see many women set free as I have taught her book *A Woman's Guide To Spiritual Warfare* in our church over the past four years. Quin comes at least once during each teaching session to share stories from her rich experience, because she says that even at age 90, she still wants to "encourage and equip" our precious women. I have all 31 of her books on my shelf at home and refer to them often as I teach. — **Jane Davis**, *Intercessor Prayer Elder, Generations United Church, Niceville, Florida*

Quin and I met in 1973 when she was visiting her mother in Destin and attended the church where we were members. She came to our home to interview me and my husband Ken, an Air Force officer who had been a prisoner of war in Vietnam 13 months. Aglow magazine published her article. Her family moved here in 1980 and for the next ten years we were close friends. Then they relocated.

When they returned to our area 20 years ago, we reconnected and began to pray for our families on a regular basis. I attended her writing seminars, and some of my articles were published in Christian magazines. The most recent one was about my experiences as a POW wife during the waiting period, 50 years after Quin first wrote our testimony. Quin still inspires me. She is unconditionally encouraging, prayerful, and supportive. She has been such a blessing to me throughout our many years of friendship. —**Anne Frasier**, *member, Immanuel Anglican Church, Destin, Florida*

I remember the day in the early 1990s when Quin walked through our doors at Victory Christian Fellowship in Somerset, Kentucky. She unlocked a world that we didn't know existed through her book *A Woman's Guide to Spiritual Warfare*. I am so grateful that our relationship continued from there. Even today—years later—our church's prayer team prays faithfully for her each week as she relays to us her prayer needs. She has continually been a mentor to me and my family, being only a phone call or email away. Mentoring is not something you can Google. It requires human dialogue. Quin has not just impacted me through the years, but she is mentoring the generation after me through me—my daughters-in-law, my grandchildren, and tons of spiritual children. Heaven will be richer because of it. —**Mrs. Jeanette Harrell**, *pastor's wife, Somerset, Kentucky*

PONDERING MY JOURNEY

Many years ago, after reading Quin's first book, *How to Pray for Your Children*, a friend and I in Lexington started a women's prayer group to do just that—pray for our children weekly. Soon our husbands joined us on Wednesday nights to pray in our home. There were 17 of us in the original group. After all these years, we still meet when needed. It really helped that Quin came periodically to our home in Kentucky to encourage us. Our dependence on God carried us through the child rearing years and established long time, loving relationships among our praying parents. Quin and I still keep up with each other by frequent phone calls and my husband Bob and I pray faithfully for her.
—**Dorothea Sims**, *Former Area Aglow officer, Lexington, Kentucky*

Ms. Quin, I want to thank you for all the times that you met with Mom and me and had conversations about writing. Also, I appreciate all the years of encouragement to write, write, write. Your encouragement to write articles, enter contests, and write my story. Write my book. And what a privilege it was to work with you on your book, *Casting Your Shadow*. As I copy-edited, it made me aware of the people who have been influential in my life and your admonition to write thank-you notes to those people pushed me to do it. It also made me conscious of how I can be an influence or a mentor for other people.

You have totally given of yourself to help other writers. You are the most diligent and prolific writer I know. You share so abundantly all you have learned from the writing life, and you impart tirelessly to others, giving a hand up and inspiration to many…

You spent years praying for me for my future husband and that prayer has been answered. Now I'm married to an amazing man, and we have a wonderful child. Thank you, from the bottom of my heart. I am so grateful for your time, encouragement, prayers, example, and leadership…Thank you. —**Désirée Schroeder**, *book editor and pastor's wife, Panama City, Florida*

Dear Miss Quin: When you began to mentor me three years ago, you said there were two things I needed to do: get a prayer partner and mentor others. I have done both. My prayer time with Anna twice a week has been one of the best possible things for my life—thank you so very much for suggesting that. We both feel it has helped our prayer lives. I have also found several creative strategies to mentor students, and I am always praying for more! God sent you into my life at exactly the right moment—to pray for me to get married (which happened a few months later!), to give me a spiritual example, and to encourage me as I published my first book, *Thomas Jefferson and His Fight Against Slavery*. Know that there's someone in Ohio who loves you and whose life you changed. Thank you! —***Dr. Cara Rogers Stevens***, *Professor, Ohio*

Quin and I spent most of a recent sunny Florida February day together, visiting places that were milestones in her life; standing in her familiar spot by the Gulf of Mexico; sitting at a picnic table in a park, asking God to give me the desires of my heart after Quin challenged me to think about my dreams.

Anyone watching us on that Thursday would have thought we were old friends. But we weren't. I met Quin Sherrer online several years ago. I had been a big fan of her writing and had reached out to her via an email I found on her blog. In my note, I mentioned writers that the Lord had directed me to: Jamie Buckingham, Derek Prince, John Sherrill, Dutch Sheets, and Catherine Marshall.

When I wrote those words, I had no idea Quin personally knew each of these giants of the faith. To me, they were legends, giants of God who through direction and inspiration of the Holy Spirit poured out their faith to and for the world.

And here I was, talking with Quin. Praying with her. Talking about books, revivals, healings, warfare, and on and on. I was awestruck that for some reason, God had placed Quin, this giant of the faith, in my path. So I followed.

It's one thing to idolize a giant of the faith. But it's another thing to laugh together with an old friend. Quin and I may have met only a few years ago, but we both know our friendship was written by the Author of Life, Himself. —***Dr. Elizabeth Patton***, *Ph.D., Professor, Applied Linguistics, University of Louisville, Kentucky*

I was young mom in my early 30s in 1999 when I heard Quin teach at the Women of Destiny conference in Van Nuys, California. As Quin spoke, the Lord began showing me what a Spirit-led life could be like. The following year, I invited Quin to minister to our very evangelical church. She was brilliant in how she created a bridge between the world of the evangelicals and the world of the charismatics. Over the years she continued to mentor me in the things of the Lord, stirring me into believing God for a greater move of His Holy Spirit. Since meeting Quin, the Lord has used me to mentor leaders and influencers in the church, the government and in the marketplace, both nationally and internationally—to see the Kingdom of God advance. I can trace all of this back to the day that God answered my prayer for a mentor, and He brought Quin into my life. I thank God for the impact she had on me then, that she continues to have on me today, and the impact she has on so many! —***Christina Horn***, *President, Shift Ministries, Alta Loma, CA.*

I remember as a small child going with Mom on some of her newspaper assignments if she was just taking photos, not doing interviews. When she photographed crowds of people watching a space launch from our town's riverbank, I was sometimes in that group waving an American flag she gave me because she was so patriotic. For her newspaper column, "Good Night, Lord," she often wrote about our life growing up—the challenges our parents faced raising the three of us such as sickness, broken bones, wrong friendships, and of course the good things that we experienced too.

Even when I became a mother myself, she was always available to come help me out if I needed her.

She prays her strong prayers for me when we talk on the phone every day. Now that she is 90, I get to help her by taking her to doctor appointments, solving her computer problems, and driving her on long rides to see the nearby white sand beaches along the Gulf of Mexico, which is one of her favorite things to do. I'm so glad I had this mom as mine to be with me on the journey of life. Her love is not just in word but in deeds. —*From her youngest daughter, Sherry*

Quin's name has been mentioned in my family's home since I was about nine years old. She became a friend and mentor to my mother, Sherry Anderson. They travelled, spoke, wrote, laughed, cried, and prayed together. The gift of writing flowed back and forth like a wave washing over them. I guess you could say the waves baptized my mother into a school run by the writing coach of all time. Quin's direct pressing on just the right points really does make you want to please her and do better for yourself. I know, because I now, too, benefit from her lessons. This is how I see our dear friend. —*Debi Fletcher*, Chipley, Florida

Words, A Tribute to Quin

—by Debi Fletcher

A word, a lesson.
A wink, then a scold.
A thought, then a novel,
A history, now a memoir.

She provokes thought never dreamed of,
And pains never pricked,
Wells of joy never tapped,
And unspeakable thoughts now have words.

How many are alive?
How many now can speak?
How many now are free,
Over crafted words with meaning?

After longing and waiting
To remember her youth,
Pen hit paper with power,
And will now bear much fruit.

I hold heart in my hand,
Now two hands gathered tightly,
She'll hear heaven call out,
Here comes one who was mighty.

Award reads: "Quin Sherrer: In grateful acknowledgment for your service to the body of Christ through your writing and influence. Deborahs United, 2021."

Saying good-bye. Quin's shadow follows her as she leaves a Christian women's conference in Texas where, at age 88, she was honored for her writing contribution. She ponders and asks, "Lord, what's next?" (Photo by Mary Jo Pierce.)

Quin's Biography & Book List

Biography of Quin Sherrer

Quin Sherrer has written or co-authored 31 books (primarily with Ruthanne Garlock) including bestsellers *A Woman's Guide to Spiritual Warfare*, *How to Pray for Your Children*, and *Miracles Happen When You Pray*.

They received an Evangelical Christian Publishers Association nomination for a "Gold Medallion Award" for *God Be With Us: A Daily Guide to Praying for Our Nation*.

She has spoken to audiences in 47 states and 12 nations, encouraging them in their daily and sometimes challenging walks of faith. As a guest on more than 375 radio and television programs—including *The 700 Club*, *100 Huntley Street*, and various shows on the Daystar Television Network and the Trinity Broadcasting Network—she's addressed topics of prayer, hospitality, miracles, personal renewal, and widowhood.

Quin holds a B.S. degree in journalism from Florida State University. She spent her early career writing for newspapers and magazines in the Cape Kennedy, Florida, area where her late husband, LeRoy, was a NASA engineer. A winner of Guideposts magazine's Writers Workshop writing contest, she was also named Writer of the Year at the Florida Writers in Touch Conference. Several of her titles have been republished by book clubs. Many are translated into other languages.

PONDERING MY JOURNEY

She has three children and six grandchildren. You can contact her through her website at www.quinsherrer.com.

Books by Quin Sherrer and Ruthanne Garlock

Becoming a Spirit-Led Mom

The Beginners Guide to Receiving the Holy Spirit

God Be with Us: A Daily Guide to Praying for Our Nation (nominated for Gold Medallion Award)

Grandma, I Need Your Prayers: Blessing Your Grandchildren Through the Power of Prayer

How to Forgive Your Children

How to Pray for Family and Friends

How to Pray for Your Children

Lord, I Need to Pray with Power

Lord, I Need Your Healing Power

The Making of a Spiritual Warrior: A Woman's Guide to Daily Victory

Prayer Partnerships: Experiencing the Power of Agreement

Prayers Women Pray: Intimate Moments with God

Praying Prodigals Home: Taking Back What the Enemy Has Stolen

The Spiritual Warrior's Prayer Guide

Warfare Prayers for Women

A Woman's Guide to Breaking Bondages

A Woman's Guide to Getting Through Tough Times

A Woman's Guide to Spirit-Filled Living

A Woman's Guide to Spiritual Warfare

You Can Break that Habit and Be Free

Books by Quin Sherrer

Good Night, Lord: Inspiration for the End of the Day

Cast Your Shadow: Influence on Purpose

PONDERING MY JOURNEY

Hope for a Widow's Heart: Encouraging Reflections for Your Journey

A House of Many Blessings: The Joy of Christian Hospitality

How to Pray for Your Children (original version)

Let's Practice Hospitality

Listen, God Is Speaking to You: True Stories of His Love and Guidance

Miracles Happen When You Pray: True Stories of the Remarkable Power of Prayer

A Mother's Guide to Praying for Your Children

Prayers from a Grandmother's Heart

The Warm and Welcome Home

Bibles Contributed to by Quin Sherrer

The Grandmother's Bible

Women of Destiny Bible: Women Mentoring Women Through the Scriptures

Other Books Contributed to by Quin Sherrer

The Deborah Company, Jane Hamon

Women of Prayer: Released to the Nations, Aglow Ministry

A Treasury of Prayer for Mothers, Helen Allingham

Manufactured by Amazon.ca
Acheson, AB